Conten

Acknowledgements

The author and publishers wish to acknowledge the following photograph sources:

Camera Press Ltd, page 127; Sally and Richard Greenhill, page 21; The Photo Source, page 43; RoSPA, page 1.

The publishers have made every effort to trace the copyright holders, but where they have failed to do so they will be pleased to make the necessary arrangements at the first opportunity.

1: Matthew, come home

BERLIE DOHERTY

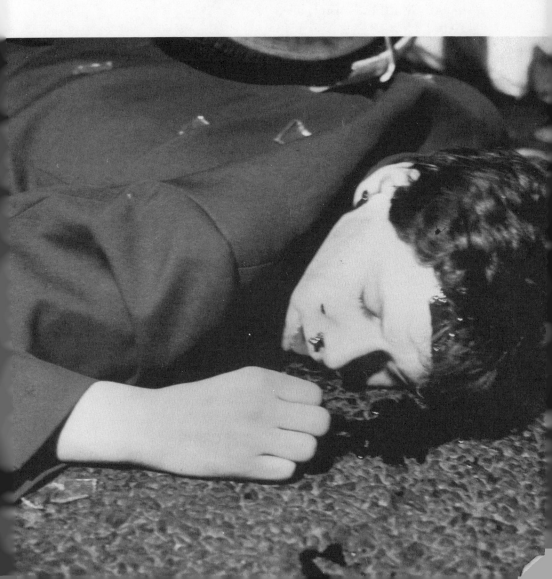

The characters

MATTHEW, aged 13
THE MAN IN GREY
KATIE, Matthew's sister, aged 18
MUM
SARAH, Matthew's sister, aged 12
DAD
SIMON, Matthew's friend, aged 13

(*Matthew is riding home from school on his bike.*)

Matthew: I hate this crossing. I'm going to have to learn how to do it, though. I can't get off my bike and walk over every time. This time I'll do it . . . No, not yet. There's a lorry coming. Now. Quick! Now . . . there's another . . . oh quick, quick.

(*Sound of brakes squealing, bike falling. Then silence.*)

Man in Grey: Ah! It's happened at last, has it? I knew this crossing would be worth watching. I've been waiting for this. Let's see, who've I got here? A boy. A boy in a bit of a state. Come on, now. Up you get.

Matthew: My head. Oh, my head!

Man in Grey: Oh, yes, it's a mess, boy. A mess of blood and bones. Don't you worry, you're in good hands with me. The very best hands. I'll get you home.

Matthew: It hurts!

Man in Grey: Of course it hurts. You mustn't expect this to be easy. Come on now.

(*Later. A grey room.*)

Man in Grey: Now, boy, let me take a look at you. Oh yes. Just right. Neither here nor there! Just the way I like them! Come on now, I should think you could open your eyes now.

Matthew: Where am I?

Man in Grey: Ah, don't ask me that. You're not lying under a lorry, which is where I saw you a few hours ago. No, you're not there.

Matthew: Then where am I?

Man in Grey: It doesn't matter where you are. You're safe. That's what matters. Safe with me. For now.

Matthew: I want to go home.

Man in Grey: Of course you do. They always do. They always want to go home. Well, I'll do what I can for you. You haven't got much time, though. The only way to do it is to mix up time, that's as much as I can say, really. Can you manage that?

Matthew: I don't know what you mean.

Man in Grey: Don't you? Not much I can do, then. (*Pause*) Well now, I've got work to do. I can't spend any more time with you. But look, you'll still feel pain for a bit. When it comes, concentrate on the pain. Don't try to get away from it. But DON'T LET IT WIN.

Matthew: Are you a doctor?

Man in Grey: A doctor? That's a strange idea. That's the last thing I'd call myself. More like a receptionist, really. I take people through the door. That one . . . that black one. That's the usual one. But sometimes through that one, the red one. Which one would you like to go through?

Matthew: I don't know. I just want to go home.

Man in Grey: I know, so you keep saying. Well, I'll let you try the red one then. I'll have a go at a time-mix for you, but I don't always get it right. Now hurry up. I've got work to do. There's been a pile-up on the motorway, I can hear the tyres squealing. I've a very good ear for things like that. Off you go. I'd better hurry.

Matthew: I don't know how to get home from here. I don't know if I can get there . . .

Man in Grey: Good gracious, of course you can get there, if you really want to. Just through that door. Up you get.

Matthew: I think I'm going to faint.

Man in Grey: I suppose I'd better help you, then. There you go. Through the door.

Matthew: Through here? But it's . . . I don't understand. I'm home.

(*Mum is in the kitchen. Sarah is in the living-room, doing her homework. Katie comes downstairs to the door.*)

Mum: There's a terrible draught. Has the front door come open, Katie?

Katie: I'll have a look. Yes, it has. That's funny.

Matthew: Hello, Katie.

Mum: I thought it might be Matthew coming back.

Matthew: It is, Mum. I'm here.

Mum: He's late, isn't he? It must be nearly five by now.

Matthew: Mum! I'm here.

Katie: He might be at Simon's.

Mum: Of course. I'd forgotten. He often calls at Simon's on a Friday.

Matthew: Stop messing about, Mum. I've been hurt . . .

Katie: It's dark already.

Mum: So it is. I really don't like him to be out in the dark.

Matthew: Mum. Mum. Look at me. Katie!

Mum: And I wanted us to have tea early tonight, too. I've a good mind to ring Simon's and tell him to send him home.

Katie: I've got to nip up to the bike shop before it closes. D'you want me to pop in for him?

Mum: Would you, Katie? I'll give him a ring, and then I'll get on with tea. Where's Sarah?

Sarah: I'm in here, Mum. Doing my homework.

Matthew: Sarah! Sarah, look at me.

Sarah: Mum. I'm cold.

Mum: It's the draught from that door. It blew open just now.

Sarah: It's freezing.

Matthew: Sarah. Please look at me.

Sarah: I've gone and left my French dictionary at Mandy's. Now what do I do?

Matthew: My head hurts so much! I'm so tired. Concentrate on the pain, he said. I can't get outside this pain . . . it hurts . . . it hurts . . .

Man in Grey: Hello there! Back again!

Matthew: You! What's happening? How did I get here again?

Man in Grey: You didn't do very well, did you? I must say I thought you'd be quicker than this. I can't let you stay here much longer, you know. There's a queue outside.

Matthew: I don't want to stay here. I want to go home.

Man in Grey: Very well, very well. You know where the door is. Off you go. And please hurry.

Matthew: A red door . . . from a room I've never seen before . . . and into . . . our hall. Mum in the kitchen getting tea ready. Dad back home, making some coffee. Sarah doing her homework by the fire. Mum! Mum!

Mum: I really can't understand why he's so late, John. Katie's going to pop in to Simon's on the way back from the shops to see if he's there, but there was no answer when I rang up just now. Where's he got to? If he's not at Simon's, then I can't think where he'll be.

Matthew: But I'm here. You must be able to see me.

Dad: Of course he'll be there. But he'll get a good telling-off when he does come in . . . staying out till teatime.

Matthew: I'd rather have a good telling-off than this, any day. I'm HERE.

Dad: Are you sure there's nothing on at school, Sarah?

Sarah: There's never anything on at school these days. Except lessons.

Mum: I don't understand it. I wish Katie had waited for you to come home now, John. She'd have been quicker in the car.

Sarah: Stop fussing, Mum. You never fuss about me like this.

Dad: That's what you think. You're a born worrier, Joan.

Mum: Anyway, after tomorrow he'll have no excuse for coming in late.

Sarah: It's gone cold again, Mum.

Mum: Yes, it has. I thought I heard the door just now, but it must have been down the road. Oh, there it is now. Matthew?

Matthew: I'm here.

Katie: It's me. There's no one in at Simon's Mum. And I only just got to the shop in time. I'll run up and hide these in my room. Is he back?

Matthew: Yes.

Mum: No. Oh, John. I'm getting worried.

Dad: Let's have tea. If he hasn't come in when I've had my tea I'll drive down to the school. Come and set the table, Sarah.

Sarah: Can I just finish this?

Dad: All right. I'll leave you in peace for a few minutes. You can wash up instead.

Matthew: Sarah.

Sarah: Freezing in here.

Matthew: Sarah, I don't know what you're all playing at, but stop it. Stop it. It's horrible.

Sarah: Colder than our classroom even. Wish Matthew would come back. He'd do my homework for me.

Matthew: Please, Sarah. Look at me.

Sarah: I just can't work when it's as cold as this. Can't think. *Noir, noire, noirs.* Before or after the noun? The black water . . .

Matthew: Give me your pen.

Sarah: Hey! What's happening?

Matthew: Now read this, read it. 'Matthew is here. I'm here.'

Sarah: Mum! Dad!

Dad: What's up, Sarah?

Sarah: I can't believe it. Look at this. My pen started moving on its own. Look! Look what it's written.

Mum: You've got *noir* in the wrong place.

Sarah: Look what it says. 'Matthew is here. I'm here.' Mum, look at it.

Dad: Don't be silly. Of course it doesn't say that. It says 'the fish swim in the black water' in very bad French.

Sarah: But look at it! Matthew wrote it. It's his handwriting . . .

Mum: Stop it, Sarah.

Dad: This isn't funny, Sarah. You're upsetting your mother.

Sarah: But that's what it says. It is! 'Matthew is . . .'

Dad: Sarah! I'm really surprised at you. Get on with your work and let me get on with setting the table. And Joan can get on with worrying. You know what she's like — but there's no need to make matters worse.

Sarah: But Dad!

Matthew: Oh no. The pain's coming back. Just when I seem to be reaching Sarah, at least . . . I feel as if I'm slipping away again. I must stay awake this time. I mustn't let the pain win. Help me, someone. Please, please help me.

Man in Grey: I'll help you.

Matthew: You!

Man in Grey: Yes. I'm afraid you're back here with me again. You don't seem to be doing very well, do you? Perhaps you don't really want to go home . . .

Matthew: I do! I'm trying to get home. Why can't I get there? Why can't they see me? It's as if I don't exist any more!

Man in Grey: I'm afraid you're in the grey world of in-between. You might make it . . . . you might not. Who can say? But you've very little time left. I really shouldn't have given you this long.

Matthew: Please can I try again?

Man in Grey: You know the way. Through the door. Are you sure you want the red one again? It would be much easier all round if you went through the black one. I should never have mentioned the red one to you really. You're obviously not strong enough.

Matthew: I am! I want to go home!
Please let it work this time. I'll go slowly, don't rush it, take my time. Open the door very gently. Our carpet. Our stairs. Mum coming out of the kitchen. And Simon! Simon's here!

Mum: Hello, Simon, love. I thought it was Katie coming in.

Simon: I'm sorry, Mrs Peace. The front door was open so I came straight in.

Mum: Who keeps leaving it open like that? We must have ghosts!

Dad: Has Matthew gone upstairs?

Simon: Matthew? I haven't come with Matthew, Mr Peace. I haven't seen him today. I didn't go to school — we've been at my Grandma's because she was ill. I've come to ask Matthew if there was any homework.

Mum: John! Now what?

Dad: I don't know, love. I felt sure he'd be with Simon.

Sarah: Mum. Something's happened to Matthew.

Dad: Stop it, Sarah. Simon, let me give you a lift home, and then I'll drive on to school and see if he's still there.

Simon: Thanks, Mr Peace. I hope he's all right.

Matthew: Simon! Surely you can see me!

Simon: Perhaps he's at Mandy's.

Sarah: Mandy's!

Simon: Well . . . he does sometimes walk her home.

Sarah: I never knew that. Wait till I see her tomorrow!

Mum: Is Mandy on the phone, Sarah?

Sarah: No. She lives in Moss Street. Number 4. Shall I go round there? I know he's not there, though.

Mum: No. I can't stand this any longer. I'll have to go myself. And if he isn't there . . . I'll ring the police.

Dad: Don't get panicky, love.

Sarah: He won't be there, Dad. He isn't at Mandy's, and he isn't at school. I know he isn't.

Dad: Don't start that again, Sarah.

Simon: Can I help you look for him, Mr Peace?

Dad: Right. Let's get going. If he turns up, Sarah, don't let him go out again.

(*Door bangs. Mum, Dad and Simon have gone.*)

Matthew: Sarah.

Sarah: It's happening again. As soon as they go, I can feel you here. You are here, aren't you?

Matthew: Yes. I'm here. Right by you. I'm here.

Sarah: I can't hear your voice, but my head's telling me what you're saying. I can't see you, but I know you're there. It's so cold here, now. Oh Matthew, come back.

Matthew: I'm trying.

Sarah: Your voice is like a whisper in my head. But it's you, I know. Tell me what's happening.

Matthew: I don't know. Whatever it is, I'm frightened. I'm frightened of slipping away again and never coming back, never, never. I'm frightened of the black door.

Sarah: What black door? Why can't I see you? What happened to you?

Matthew: I was on my way home from school. I must have crashed into a car and come off my bike . . .

Sarah: You did what?

Matthew: I came off my bike. I smashed my head . . .

Sarah: You haven't got a bike.

Matthew: My bike. The bike I got for my birthday last week.

Sarah: Matthew. Your birthday is tomorrow.

Matthew: But I got a bike. A blue bike. You gave me a saddle-bag. Katie got me some lights . . .

Sarah: Your bike is in the garage. It's still got cardboard and wrappings round it. Katie's been up to the bike-shop to get the lights now. I've got your saddle-bag hidden under my bed . . .

Matthew: But I was riding it, Sarah! I was at that crossing up near Simon's. I crashed into something. My head was all blood and bones, the man said . . .

Sarah: What man?

Matthew: The grey man. I thought he was a doctor, but he said that was the last thing he'd call himself. He said I mustn't let the pain win, but every time it comes I seem to drift away and then I'm in his grey room on the other side of our door . . . a big, cold, grey room with a black door on one wall and a red door on the other. I can't escape, Sarah. I can get through the red door into here but I can't come back home. Nobody can see me.

Sarah: But I know you're here! Surely if I can hear you, there must be a way of bringing you back.

Matthew: I can't help myself. When the pain comes I drift away again. It's coming again now. I can't help it, Sarah. I don't know if I can come back through the door again. I can't do it on my own. Help me, Sarah. It's something to do with time, he said. Mixing up time . . .

Sarah: I want to help you, Matthew.
Mixing up time? But time's already mixed up . . . you're in a different time from me. My time is today, and your birthday is tomorrow. But why aren't you home? And your time is next week . . . you've already had your birthday . . . you've had your bike . . . and a terrible thing has happened to you. How can I stop the terrible thing from happening? Unless . . . unless I stop tomorrow! I know! I know! It might work!

(*She runs out.*)

Man in Grey: She knows what to do. Pity she's left it so late.

Matthew: You again. Please let me go.

Man in Grey: I could let you go one way, and that would be for eternity. I could let you go another way, and that would be home again, if you were strong enough to get there. I don't think you are. You've no time left, Matthew.

Matthew: Can't I just go back once more? Just to say goodbye?

Man in Grey: One last time. There's nothing more I can do for you. Time's slipping back, boy. Go on. Go on.

Matthew: I'm coming home from school. I'm running up the road. I'm pushing open the door. Please! Please!

Mum: Hello, Matthew! Good, I'm glad you're back early. I've got to go out tonight.

Katie: I'm going up to the shops, Mum. I want to get the you-know-what for tomorrow.

Mum: Wait till your dad comes in, Katie. He might let you take the car. This'll be him now. Heavens. What was that?

Katie: Sounds as if he's run over a load of tin cans.

Dad (*Outside*): Joan!

Mum: Go and see what he wants, Matthew. Oh, wait . . . you'd better not go in the garage . . .

Dad: Joan! Some stupid fool has left that bike in the middle of the garage floor, and I've just reversed the car over it. It was lying on the floor . . . right in the middle. It's ruined!

Matthew: My bike!

Dad: I'm sorry, Matthew. I didn't know you were there. That was your birthday surprise for tomorrow. You might as well come and look at it . . . but you'll never ride it now, I'm afraid. It's just a mess of metal and rubber.

Katie: Saved me a journey, anyway. I was just going up to get you some lights for it.

Sarah: Oh, Matthew. Your lovely bike. I'm sorry.

Matthew: Thanks, Sarah.

Sarah: What d'you mean, thanks! I don't know anything about it, anyway. I've been trying to do my French homework. Want to help me?

Man in Grey: Matthew!

Matthew: No! What do you want?

Man in Grey: I just want to say — goodbye!

Matthew: It's cold out here. Let's go in, shall we? I'm starving!

Activities

Matthew, come home is written as a radio play. Before you present a reading of it, or make a tape-recording of it, first work through these exercises.

Thinking about the characters

1 Think about Matthew's family as a whole. What impression did you form of his family and their home? What sort of street do they live in? What is their home like? What sort of car do they have? Write down your ideas about Matthew's family, their house and their car. Then, either write a brief description saying what you think their living room is like or draw a sketch or a plan of it. When you have finished, form groups and compare your ideas about Matthew's family and their home.

2 Now, think about each member of the family. Work in groups of five. Each take one member of the family and prepare a statement about that person to present in role to the other members of the group. Say what your interests are, what job you do or hope to do, what sort of person you are and what your feelings are about the other members of the family.

3 Make a 'feelings chart'. Divide a piece of paper into six columns. At the top of the left-hand column, write 'Scene'. At the top of the other five columns, write the names of Matthew's family. Next, in the left-hand column make a list of the scenes that occur in the play. Then, think about each scene in turn, and in the other columns write down what the feelings are of the characters who appear in that scene.

4 Talk about the Man in Grey.
   a) Who is he? What does he represent?
   b) What impression of the Man in Grey would you try to create if you were playing that part? How would you speak his lines? What sort of voice would you use? Soft? Harsh? Oily? Husky? Strident? Deep? On a piece of paper write down what sort of voice you would use and why. Then, form groups and discuss how you would portray the Man in Grey.

Thinking about the situations

Role-play the following scenes.

Further developments

1 'I don't know what you mean.' At the end of the play, when Matthew thanks Sarah, she says: 'I don't know anything about it.' Is she just covering up or has any recollection of the events been wiped from her mind? Role-play a scene later that evening when Matthew is alone with Sarah and he talks to her about the unusual experience he has had. How does Sarah respond?

2 'Tell me about your experience.' In pairs, act out a scene in which a person who investigates paranormal experiences talks to Matthew and asks him questions about his experience. Before you begin, make a list of questions that the investigator is going to ask.

Parallel situations

1 'Sarah, where are you?' Work in a group. Develop a playlet involving the same characters. This time it is Sarah who is in some kind of danger. She tries to contact the family so that they can come to her aid. Only Matthew can sense that she is trying to contact them.

2 'Don't go. Please don't go.' A girl or a boy, who has had a premonition that it is dangerous for a sister or a brother to go somewhere tries to warn her/him and to persuade her/him not to go.

Presenting the play

1 Work in groups of seven and prepare either a reading or a tape-recording of the play. Simon only appears in one scene, so the person who plays the part of Simon can be in charge of producing the sound effects and making the tape-recording.

Before you begin, think about how you are going to indicate to your audience that a scene-change has taken place. When you come to each scene-change, experiment with different ways of indicating it, e.g. a pause, sound effects, fading voices out and in, or a few bars of music.

Think too about how you could use music to create the right
sort of atmosphere at the beginning and end of this play. Can
anyone in the group suggest a suitable piece of music you could
use? Or perhaps you could use a synthesiser to produce an
appropriate piece of electronic music? Decide what sort of
music you need and what kind of atmosphere you want to
create, then try out different pieces until you find a suitable
one.

2 a) Although this was written as a radio play, it could be
presented as a stage play. It would be important to make the
action of the play continuous, so there are a number of
problems you would have to solve. For example, how would
you present the accident at the start of the play? How would
you arrange the set so that Matthew could move swiftly
between the grey room and his home? How would you present
the Man in Grey, so as to make him a paranormal figure? In a
group, talk about these and any other problems you would face
in putting on a stage production of the play. Then, compare
your solutions to the problems with the solutions other groups
suggest.

b) Design a set for *Matthew, come home,* showing how you
would use the space on your stage or in your drama studio, if
you were directing a stage production of the play.

Writing your own scripts

1 In *Matthew, come home* time is mixed up and Matthew is
involved in a timeslip, but the play has quite a simple
structure. With the exception of the accident at the start of the
play, all the action takes place either in the grey room or in
Matthew's home. Write a script of your own centred on a
timeslip, in which the action shifts backwards and forwards
between just two locations.

2 'It's up to you.' Work with a partner. Write a script about a teenager who has a difficult decision to make, because some friends are pressurising her/him to do something and she/he cannot decide whether or not to do it. Develop your script so that the action moves between a darkened room and the real world, just as the action in *Matthew, come home* moves between the grey room and the real world. In the darkened room, show the teenager trying to decide what to do in the course of conversations with a figure dressed in legal robes and a wig, who represents her/his conscience. One way of developing your script would be to show the different scenes that could develop in the real world, depending on which decision the teenager makes.

2: That's a funny name

DAVID WILLIAMS

The characters

SALLY, aged 13
ZAHID, aged 13
DAD, Sally's father
PETER, aged 15

(*A classroom door opens.*)

Sally: You know you're not supposed to be in here?

Zahid: This is my classroom.

Sally: Yeah, but . . .

(*Closer*)

You're the new one, aren't ya?

Zahid: Please?

Sally: The new boy what started this morning?

Zahid: Yes.

Sally: Only you're supposed to go out at lunchtimes. It's the rule. Not that I'm bothered, but I'm corridor monitor this week so I'm supposed to make sure everybody's out, see.

Zahid: I see.

Sally: So . . .

Zahid: Can I stay here?

Sally: Well, it's the rule . . .

Zahid: I'd rather stay here, if that's all right.

Sally: It isn't really, not if the teacher comes along. It's not raining or anything. You cold? I mean it's not cold out, but if you're used to sunshine . . .

Zahid: No. I'm British, you know. I've always lived in England.

Sally: Really? Well . . . do you like it here?

Zahid: Here?

Sally: In . . . No, that's a daft question in't it, if you've always . . . What's your name?

Zahid: Zahid.

Sally: That's a funny name. I'm Sally. You frightened they'll give you the bumps?

Zahid: The bumps?

Sally: They always scare new ones with the bumps. It's not bad, though. I had 'em when I came. Reckoned they were gonna stick my head down the loo an' all sorts, but they never did. The bumps aren't so bad, honest. Have you just moved round here?

Zahid: Yes.

Sally: Where d'you live?

Zahid: Mmm . . .

Sally: Can't remember?

Zahid: I . . . can't remember the name of the street.

Sally: Hope you don't get lost going home. Is it far?

Zahid: Just at the corner of . . . No, it's not far.

Sally: Hey, it's not your family what's opened up shop where Miller's used to be? My dad said some Pakis had taken over Miller's. Are you a Paki?

Zahid: I'm British. My . . . parents come from Pakistan.

Sally: Thought so. You're the only one in our year.
Is that you, then, what's opened up the corner shop?

Zahid: Please don't tell anybody.

Sally: Don't tell anybody? Why not?

Zahid: Please don't . . .

Sally: All right. Just as you like.

(*The bell rings.*)

Listen to that. You've kept us talking so's I wouldn't throw you out.

Zahid: Thank you.

Sally: 'S all right. Enjoyed it. See you round.

Zahid: See you.

(*Fade. Fade in sound of TV.*)

Dad: (*In another room*) Sal?

Sally: What?

Dad: We're out of milk.

Sally: What?

Dad (*Closer*):   We're out of milk. Nip down the shop an' get some, will ya?

Sally: I'm watching this.

Dad: It's only adverts. Go on, just take you a minute.

Sally: It's after eight. They won't be open.

Dad: Yeah, they will. That new Paki shop will. They're open all hours. Go on.

Sally: I won't. Why d'you keep calling it the Paki shop?

Dad: That's what it is.

Sally: If it was Welsh people in there you wouldn't call it the Welsh shop, would ya? Or the Geordie shop if it was people from Newcastle? They've got names, you know.

Dad: Not above the door they haven't. It's still Miller's over the door. I don't know what they're called.

Sally: You could ask. Anyway, the boy's called Zahid. He's nice. Here, gimme the money. I'll go.

Dad: Oh, right. Mind they give you fresh . . .

(*Door closes.*)

Changeable as the wind, that one. Can't make her out sometimes . . .

(*Fade. Shop bell tinkles.*)

Sally: Hi, Zahid.

Zahid: Oh. Hello.

Sally: Got any milk?

Zahid: Mmm, yes. Pint?

Sally: Please. You've got this place looking smart. Them Millers was scruffy.

Zahid: My mother worked very hard cleaning it all up.

Sally: Wish we had a shop. Your family must have plenty of money.

Zahid: No, honestly.

Sally: Why don't you want people to know your dad's got a shop? I'd be braggin' if it were me . . .

Zahid: No. People don't like it. Last place we lived in kids would ... Quick, my father's coming. Take the milk. Goodbye.

Sally: What ...?

Zahid: Goodbye. Thank you.

Sally: I haven't paid.

Zahid: It's OK. On the house. See you.

(*Shop bell rings.*)

Sally: Well, you're a funny one, Zahid what's-your-name ...

(*Shop bell rings again as the door closes. Cross-fade to ringing of school bell, followed by sound of released teenagers running, breaking free through the school gates.*)

Sally: Hey, Zahid! Zahid! Wait for me.

(*Running*)

Wait on. What you in such a hurry for?

Zahid: Sorry, I didn't see you. I'm just trying to get home ...

Sally: *Trying* to get home? You say some daft things. Slow down, will ya? What's the big rush? I'd like to walk along wi' you if you don't mind. An' I mean *walk*.

Zahid: I'll have to get back to the shop ...

Sally: Your dad makes you work too hard. If it were me I'd tell 'im where to get off. How much does he pay ya?

Zahid: He doesn't pay me. It's expected ...

Sally: He's got no right to expect anything. You've got your school work to do. That's what I tell mine. Since Mam left he expects me to cook an' clean, the lot. I just tell 'im ...

Zahid: 'Scuse, Sally. Got to go!

Sally: Where you off?

Peter: Paki! Wanna word wi' you. Come 'ere!

Sally: What's goin' on?

Peter: Been looking for you.

Sally: Leave off 'im, that's a new jacket.

Peter: It's you's got the corner shop, in't it?

Zahid: Not me.

Peter: Tells lies an' all, like all the Pakis.

Sally: I know you, Pete Watson. Pick on somebody your own size.

Peter: An' you better pick on one your own colour. Goin' round wi' foreigners . . .

Sally: He's not foreign, he's British. Anyway, what's it to you?

Peter: I don't like 'em. Nobody likes 'em. Coming in pinching us jobs. Takin' over us shops . . .

Sally: You never owned Miller's.

Peter: Where'd he get money for a shop?

Sally: Tell 'im, Zahid.

Zahid: My dad saved it.

Sally: His dad saved it, see. What'd *your* dad ever do but get chucked outa pubs?

Peter: I'll bray you!

Sally: Run, Zahid!

Zahid: Run, Sally!

Sally: I'm running!

(*Fade running. Fade in running, different surface. Scuffle stop.*)

Sally (*Panting*): Here, get in!

Zahid (*Panting*): Can't, Sally. Have to . . .

Sally: Don't argue.

(*Door slams. Interior acoustic.*)

God, I'm dead. We left 'im standin' though, eh?

Zahid: Never ran so fast. And I've had some practice.

Sally: You a runner, then?

Zahid: Like a hare when the white fox is after me.

Sally: You what?

Dad (*Off*): That you, Sal? (*Closer*) Oh!

Sally: Dad, this is Zahid. He's come for tea.

(*Sounds of plates in a sink; running water.*)

Sally (*Confidentially*): Well?

Dad: Well what?

Sally: What d'you think of 'im?

Dad: He never touched that bacon. Lovely bit o' bacon that, an' he never touched it.

Sally: Mebbe he's not fond o' bacon.

Dad: He could've tried a bit, just to be polite.

Sally: Don't talk to me about polite. You've never said a word to 'im yet. That's not very polite.

Dad: Well, I can't think of anything. I don't know what they talk about.

Sally: Just the same as us. You sound like that Pete Watson.

Dad: I've got nothing against the lad . . .

Sally: Well, talk to 'im, then. Make 'im feel at home. Go on, while I finish these dishes off.

Dad: I'll do 'em.

Sally: That's a turn-up for the books. Should bring Zahid home every day. Go on, get in there.

Dad (*Grumbling as he goes*): You're worse than your mother sometimes.

(*Opening the door he changes to a note of forced cheeriness.*)

Aye-aye!

Zahid: Hello.

Dad: Would you like anything else, er . . . ?

Zahid: No, thank you.

Dad: Biscuit or summat?

Zahid: No.

Dad: They're from your shop, them biscuits. We buy quite a bit from Miller's as was. Very handy, specially on Sundays an' that. He works long shifts, your dad. Does he get out much?

Zahid: Sorry?

Dad: I've never seen 'im down at the local.

Zahid: No.

Dad (*In a burst of confidence*): Tell 'im if he wants a pint or two anytime I'll keep 'im company.

Zahid: Well . . . (*Door opens.*)

Dad: Here, Sally, I'm just telling . . . your pal here that if his dad ever fancies a pint I'll take 'im round to The Lion.

Sally: Any excuse.

Dad: Don't forget to tell 'im.

Sally: It would be a break from the shop.

Zahid: My father doesn't drink . . . alcohol.

Dad: Oh. (*Pause*) Just a thought.

Zahid: I'm sorry, I really will have to go. I'm supposed to be at the shop now. Thank you for the tea.

Sally: Hang on, I'll walk down with ya.

Zahid: I'll have to run.

Sally: I'll run down wi' you, then. You don't get rid o' me that easy.

(*Fade. Exterior acoustic. A car goes by.*)

Zahid: Goodnight, Sally. Thanks again for the tea.

Sally: I'll see you across the road.

Zahid: No. No, please don't. I'd rather say goodbye here.

Sally: What's the matter wi' you?

Zahid: My father . . .

Sally: Yeah, I knew that was it. You don't want your dad to see me, do ya?

Zahid: No, but . . .

Sally: Look, I know I'm not the best-dressed lass in school, but I'm not scruffy . . .

Zahid: That's not . . .

Sally: Poor but clean. You don't have to be ashamed o' me.

Zahid: You don't understand . . .

Sally: Yeah, I do. Your dad'll think I'm not good enough for you in that nice new uniform an' the way you talk proper an' him wi' a shop an' me just a lass from the back streets . . .

Zahid (*Laughing*):   Oh, Sally!

Sally: What?

Zahid: I like you. See you tomorrow.

Sally: Come back, you! I'm not finished . . .

Zahid (*From across the road*):   Goodnight!

Sally: Ooh, I'll never understand you . . . Pakis!

(*Interior acoustic. TV noise. From outside the room the sound of a front door opening and closing.*)

Dad: Sal!

(*Room door opens.*)

Sally: Hi.

Dad: The wanderer returns. Since when did it take this long to walk to the corner and back?

Sally: I've been to the library.

Dad: You been where? You're not even a member.

Sally: Well, they don't throw you out. Anyway, I joined. Here, you've to sign this card.

Dad: Not if it costs.

Sally: It doesn't.

Dad: What you been down there for? You're not one for book-reading.

Sally: I been looking summat up. I needed to find out more about 'em since *he* tells you nothing.

Dad: Find out about who?

Sally: P for Pakistanis. That's where I started in this book the library woman showed us. Then I went to M for Muslims.

Dad: That's cloth, in't it?

Sally: It's a sort o' religion, stupid. It's what most Pakistanis are. Only it's not like going to church on a Sunday an' that's it for the week. It's like a whole life wi' them an' there's lots o' rules. Things you have to do, things you can't do. Should I tell you summat you didn't know about Muslims?

Dad: I don't know nowt about 'em.

Sally: I'll tell you two things. Number one, they don't eat pigs. It's against their religion.

Dad: Oh. Your pal's a Muslin, is he?

Sally: Muslim. Yeah, I reckon he is.

Dad: No wonder he didn't touch that bacon.

Sally: And number two, they're not allowed to drink alcohol. So you see, Zahid's dad's not being unfriendly, he's just being . . .

Dad: Religious.

Sally: Right. See, they're very strict about it.

Dad: Loonies, if you ask me.

Sally: Just different. Brought up different. It's really interestin' about their customs an' that.

Do you know . . . ?

Dad: D'you know I'm trying to watch this programme?

Sally: There's somethin' . . . I'm sure they mustn't do it in this country. Not these days. I must ask Zahid tomorrow . . .

(*Fade. Exterior acoustic; playground noises in the distance.*)

Zahid: You've learned a lot, Sally, in a short time.

Sally: I wanted to know. Find out about you. Are your folks strict Muslims, then?

Zahid: My father is. He gets worse as he gets older.

Sally: Worse? You make it sound like summat bad. What's wrong wi' being religious?

Zahid: I didn't mean it like that. There's nothing wrong with it. My father always tries to do things for the best. But this is a . . . different country.

Sally: How d'ya mean?

Zahid: Oh, it's hard to explain. You'd think Britain . . . Everybody says it's a free country. You can think what you like, say what you want . . . but people don't like you to be different.

Sally: That's right enough.

Zahid: But it's me too. I don't want to be different. Now, my brother. He's not like me, he's happy going to the mosque, reading the Koran . . .

Sally: That's like the Bible, in't it?

Zahid: Sort of.

Sally: Is he older than you, your brother?

Zahid: Mmm. That's it, see, Sally. He was born in Pakistan. Being a Muslim is right for him. But me . . . I've never even been there. It's just . . . it's so hard to explain. I love my family and what they believe is fine by me. But I feel . . . I just want to be an ordinary English boy. The thing is, people don't let you.

Sally: People like Pete Watson?

Zahid: Yes.

Sally: We're not all like that, you know.

Zahid: I know, Sally. But there's my parents too. They are always telling me that Pakistan is my true home and I should try to be a good Muslim.

Sally: Do you have rows about it?

Zahid: Used to. They only made things worse. These days I just try to keep quiet, keep things hidden.

Sally: Me, for instance.

Zahid: I suppose so.

Sally: Your dad wouldn't like me, would he?

Zahid: Not as . . . you know.

Sally: Zahid, in this book it said that Muslims go in for arranged marriages.

Zahid: That's right.

Sally: Is that where you marry somebody you've maybe never even met before the wedding, like kings an' high people used to do in olden times?

Zahid: A bit like that. The parents fix it up usually.

Sally: Not these days though, eh? Not here?

Zahid: It happens. My father has already started to talk . . .

Sally: He wouldn't! He couldn't do that here, it wouldn't be allowed.

Zahid: Happens every day.

Sally: But what if you didn't like each other? (*Pause*) And Zahid . . . what if . . . what if when we got older we wanted to get married?

Zahid (*Laughing*): Sally!

Sally: No, but it could happen one day, couldn't it? You never know. What if it did?

Zahid: There'd be a big fight. My family, your family . . . Great big fight. And we would be in the middle of it.

Sally: What would you do?

Zahid: What I always do when a fight starts. Run away.

Sally: Could I run with you?

Zahid: I'd like you to.

Sally: I will, then. (*Pause*) Talking about fights, look who's coming over.

Zahid: Pete Watson. Let's run, Sally!

Sally: Hang on. I've got this book in my bag. Brought it in specially for Pete Watson.

Zahid: *Asians In Britain.* You won't get him to read that. His sort will never under . . .

Sally: Who said owt about reading? This book's just a nice size for banging over 'is head. Come on, Zahid. It's *our* turn. GERONIMO . . . !

(*Fade on Sally's battle-cry.*)

Activities

That's a funny name is a radio play, written to be read aloud and tape-recorded, rather than to be presented on stage. Before you make a tape-recording of the play, first work through these exercises.

Thinking about the characters

Sally

1   What sort of a person is Sally? What do you learn about her from the way she behaves towards a) Zahid b) Pete c) her dad? Is she the sort of person you would like to have as a friend? Give your reasons.

2   Try to convey your impression of Sally by writing a thumbnail sketch of her. Think about what you learned about her and her background from the play. Then use your imagination to fill in other details. For example, what is her home like? What is her bedroom like? What does she spend her time doing? What are her interests? How well does she get on at school? Write down your ideas about Sally, then compare them with other people's.

3 Imagine you are Sally. Write two or three diary entries in which you tell your diary about your meetings with Zahid and your thoughts about your conversations with him. Then form groups and discuss what you have written.

Zahid

1 Talk about how Zahid behaves when he first meets Sally. Why is he so defensive? Why doesn't he want anyone to know that his family have taken over the corner shop?

2 a) Imagine you are Zahid. Write down what your thoughts and feelings were during the scene with Pete.

b) Discuss what you have written and say how you would have behaved if you had been Zahid.

3 a) How does Zahid try to stop his family finding out about his friendship with Sally? Talk about why he doesn't want them to know about it.

b) What is Zahid's attitude towards his family's culture?

4 Zahid says: 'I just want to be an ordinary English boy.' Which makes it more difficult for him to be accepted as one — the attitudes of other children or the attitude of his own family?

5 You are Zahid. Write a letter to a penfriend telling him all about Sally and the difficulties you are having settling in at your new school and in a new area. Then form groups and discuss your letters. Which letter expresses most clearly the problem Zahid faces and how he feels?

Dad

1 a) What impression do you get of Sally's dad from the way he speaks to Sally and to Zahid?

b) What sort of relationship does he appear to have with Sally?

2 What picture did you form of Sally's dad? If you were putting on a stage presentation of the play, what clothes would he wear? Either draw a picture of him or write a description of the clothes you picture him wearing.

Peter

1 a) Why does Peter start bullying Zahid?

b) What do you learn about Peter as a person from the way he treats Zahid?

2 How much does Peter understand Zahid's family and their culture? Talk about why Peter and others like him are prejudiced against people like Zahid.

Thinking about the situations

Role-play the following scenes. After each scene, talk about how you showed the people behaving and say why you think they would behave in that way.

Further developments

1 'Here, you're not friendly with *him*, are you?' Another person in Sally's year has seen Sally with Zahid. She/he expresses surprise. How does Sally react? What does she say to the other person about Zahid? Role-play the scene that develops.

2 'You're just prejudiced, you are! You should read this!' Work in groups of three. Develop the scene that follows the end of the play, in which Sally and Zahid stand up to Pete. Produce a script of the scene and either tape-record it or present it to the rest of the class.

Parallel situations

1 A girl or boy, who has made friends with someone from a different cultural background, talks to a parent, just as Sally tries to talk to her dad, and explains how the new friend's family has different customs and beliefs. (Note: if necessary, prepare for this role-play by going to the library to find information, in the way that Sally did.)

2 'You're just prejudiced, you are! You should read this!' Work in groups of three. Develop the scene that follows the end of suggesting, because the custom or religion of her/his family won't allow it.

3 Like many plays, *That's a funny name* is based on a real-life experience. David Williams wrote the play about Zahid and his dilemma because he actually knows a boy with a problem just like Zahid's. Role-play a scene in which a girl or a boy with a similar problem talks about it to a friend.

Presenting the play

Work in groups of four. Put on a performance of the play either by tape-recording it or giving a reading of it to the rest of the class. The person who takes the part of Peter can be in charge of making the recording and producing the sound effects.

Writing your own scripts

1 Study the structure of the play. It consists of a number of short scenes. The changes in time and place between the scenes are indicated either by fading out the sound of the voices at the end of a scene and/or by the use of sound effects. Draw a flow chart showing the structure of the play, scene by scene, and how the link between each scene is made. Here is the start of such a chart:

Scene 1
Place : *A school classroom*
Time : *The lunch-hour*
Action: *Sally meets Zahid for*
          the first time.

Fade. Fade in
sound of TV.

2 Work in groups of five or six. Develop your own play about a gang of children and a newcomer, who is different from them in some way. Either work out your own plot or develop a series of scenes showing how the gang at first reject the newcomer, then, because of something that happens, alter their attitude towards her/him. Draw a flow chart to help you to plan your scenes. Try out your ideas as improvisations, before writing your scripts.

3: Don't look down

GARETH OWEN

For my godchildren
Robin
and Adam and Carrie

Don't look down was first produced at Watermill Primary
School, Selly Oak, Birmingham. Directed by Pauline
Woodhead.

The characters

ERIC ASHBY as an adult
ERIC ASHBY as a boy
MISS MEACHER, Head Mistress, in her fifties; severe and matriarchal
TREVOR SERGEANT (Sago)
JACKY CROPPER, a larger boy: a boxer
TRASK, Cropper's sidekick
SANDRA LINAKER, pretty. (Her description may be modified to suit the actress who plays her.)
PHYLLIS SIDEBOTHAM, fatter, wears spectacles
IRENE OLLERENSHAW
MORPETH, a more studious boy, wears spectacles
MR DEXTER, class-teacher of Class 4. Walks with a stick sometimes; short hair, moustache
DENISE
The BOYS AND GIRLS of Mary Street School

The action takes place in the hall, classrooms and playground of Mary Street Junior School. The name of the school and the location may be altered for the purposes of lending local relevance. The time is 1948 and the children should be dressed and have their hair cut accordingly.

The action of the play should appear to be continuous, rather like that of a film. As the lights fade on one scene the sound effects for the following scene can begin.

There should be no attempt to make the play a comedy. The events that are visited on the characters are serious and very real. Thus the parts must be played with a reverence for that reality. There must be no indication from the actors that they are taking part in a comedy. Any humour that resides in the play must arise naturally out of the action.

The play will be most successful if played on a composite set with perhaps a slightly raised area to one side for the classroom. Desks, benches and blackboards will do much to create a feeling of school. Ideally the parts of the adults should be played by adults.

In the stage directions, 'Right' means right as seen from the point of view of the actor looking out at the audience. Left likewise.

(*House lights fade to blackout. Children's voices sing softly.*)

All: When I was a young child
        A young child, a young child
        When I was a young child
        How happy was I.
        Singing this way and that way
        And this way and that way
        And this way and that way went I.

(*As the children's voices hum the melody softly in the background, we hear the voice of Ashby as an adult, on tape, over the loudspeakers.*)

Ashby's adult voice: I read in the paper last week that my old Headmistress was ill in hospital. Her name was Miss Meacher.

(*Spotlight up on Miss Meacher sitting upright centre.*)

Meacher: Rose Ann Meacher. My father always called me Rose. I expect the children called me something else.

(*Lights up on all the children. There could be up to twenty-five. They are lined up looking straight out as though for a school photograph. Ashby, Sergeant and Cropper are on the back row right. Sandra and Phyllis need to be removed from them and to*

*the left. The photographer has to be imagined as though he were in
the audience area. Mr Dexter at times busies himself, checking
with the photographer and seeing the children are straight. When
he sits, his place is on a chair to Meacher's left.)*

All: Old Miss Meacher
Our Headteacher
Fell in the lav
And no one could reach her.

Ashby's adult voice: Everybody was scared of her. Even my
dad and Mr Dexter were scared of her.

Meacher: Eric Ashby, is that you talking?

(The boy Ashby's head whips round.)

Ashby's adult voice: Yes, Miss Meacher, I'm still talking.

Meacher: I taught your father, Ashby. He was just the same.

Ashby's adult voice: I thought of her lying in a hospital bed.
I thought, 'No one's scared of you any more, Miss Meacher.'

Sandra: She never got married.

Phyllis: Never had no children

Trask: She'll die on her own.

Denise: The caretaker will come.

Irene: And turn off the school lights.

All: *(Chanting or singing. Not hard. A sad tune would make a
useful contrast with the harshness of the words.)*

Never had a boyfriend
Never no one's wife
Lived in a school desk all her life.

Sleeps on a blackboard
Drinks school ink
Washes her hair
In the old school sink.

Ashby's adult voice: I didn't think she'd remember me.

Meacher: Of course I remember you. I remember everybody. You remember I called you The Lapwing.

Ashby's adult voice: Lapwing?

Meacher: Remember?
He who fights and runs away

All: Lives to fight another day.

Meacher: Eric Ashby, are you listening?

(*Ashby's head is looking left.*)

Ashby's adult voice: That's me there, not looking at the camera. I'm looking at Sandra Linaker.

Sandra: Sandra Ann Felicity Linaker. Eleven years old, blonde hair, violet eyes. They say I'm the prettiest girl in the school. When I grow up I'm going to call myself Angelique.

Ashby's adult voice: I was in love with Sandra Linaker.

Meacher: Eric Ashby, are you listening to me? Have you combed your hair this morning?

Ashby: Ain't got no comb, miss.

Meacher: There's no such word as ain't.

Dexter: Haven't got a tie on either, have you, Ashby?

Meacher: Every boy was told distinctly to wear a tie for the school photograph.

Ashby: Miss, I thought . . . . . .

Meacher: Thought! Thought! We all know what thought did, don't we?

All: Followed a dust cart and thought it was a wedding.

Dexter: He'd forget his brain if it was loose.

Cropper: What brain?

(*Laughter*)

Meacher: Who said that? Mr Dexter, who said that?

Dexter: Cropper, Miss Meacher.

Meacher: I might have known. Jacky Cropper, what makes you imagine for one moment that I want to hear your opinion?

Cropper: Miss, I thought . . . .

Meacher: We know what thought did, don't we?

All: Followed a dust cart . . .

Meacher: That will do!
Now, I've gone to a great deal of trouble and expense to have this school photograph taken. And it's not for my benefit you know. Phyllis Sidebotham, I'm sure Sandra Linaker is capable of combing her own hair. Trouble and expense; so, I want no one moving. Perfectly still. Is that clear? Are we ready, Mr Dexter?

Meacher: Very well. On the count of three all shout out Wensleydale and hold it. Hold your breaths and freeze. We all know what freeze means, don't we?

All: Yes, Miss Meacher.

Meacher: Ready? One-Two, Ashby eyes front — what are you looking at?

Cropper: We know.

Meacher: One.

Ashby: Shut up, Crophead.

Meacher: Two.

(*Dexter runs back from the 'camera' and sits, arms folded, next to Meacher.*)

Cropper: Looking at Sandra Linaker.

Meacher: Three.

Cropper: Pass it on — Ashby's in love with Sandra Linaker.

All: WENSLEYDALE.

(*All freeze and smile.*)

Ashby: Shut up, you, Cropper. (*He pushes him.*)

(*Blackout. Camera clicks. Lights on. All freeze. White light comes on. We see everybody still, smiling, except for Cropper who has his mouth open and his arms in the air and is leaning precipitously sideways.*
Hold for three seconds and then blackout.)

Ashby's adult voice: What I couldn't remember was why she called me Lapwing. I couldn't remember that. Lapwing. What was that? I meant to write and ask her. But three days later it was too late.

(*Bell rings loudly. Blackout.*)

Meacher: Who said you could move? Go back to your desks.

(*Lights up. Miss Meacher at a blackboard.*)

That bell is for me, not for you. Perfectly still. Absolutely silent. I should be able to hear a pin drop. (*Pause. Silence.*) That's better.

Now, here is our Handwriting Exercise for today. Let me hear you all read it.

All: Today's lesson from Mother Nature in her Wisdom.

Meacher: Sandra Linaker. The first sentence.

Sandra: Nature is full of lovely things which we can observe and learn from. Today's lesson comes from the lapwing.

Meacher: Phyllis Sidebotham.

Phyllis: The lapwing is a frequent and welcome visitor to these shores. He is a member of the plover family.

Meacher: Trevor Sergeant.

Sergeant: Also he his . . .

Meacher: He is . . .

Sergeant: He is, er, known as the pee twit.

(*The class giggles.*)

Meacher: That'll do. I do not consider an inability to read simple English to be a cause for merriment. What's that word, Sergeant?

Sergeant: Pee wit, miss.

Cropper: Sergeant's the Pee twit.

(*Laughter from the class.*)

Meacher: Irene Ollerenshaw.

Irene: He is a-p-p-r-p . . .

Meacher: Who can tell her?

Morpeth: He is appropriately called wit because he uses his wits to protect himself and his fledglings. Should a thoughtless wanderer stray near his nest, instead of fighting he moves away crying, thereby distracting the enemy from the vulnerable fledglings.

Meacher: Beautifully read, Andrew Morpeth. A point for Scott house.

Now, who can think of an appropriate proverb for the pee wit?

Morpeth: Miss. Miss.

Meacher: Ashby.

Ashby: Erm. A, er . . . like a stitch in what-you-call-it.

Irene: Don't know, miss.

Morpeth: Miss, miss.

Meacher: Morpeth?

Morpeth: He who fights and runs away lives to fight another day.

Meacher: Good. Now remember, if you have your polyphotos for the school magazine bring them tomorrow.

Sandra: Miss, I brought mine today.

Meacher: Well, keep it safe in your desk, Sandra. Eric Ashby, stay behind and finish copying the text. The rest of you can go. You too, Sergeant.

(*Meacher walks out. The rest exit noisily. Ashby and Sergeant are left.*)

Sergeant: Always picks on me.

Ashby: Keep look-out.

Sergeant: What you doing, Ashy?

(*Ashby goes to Sandra's desk. Opens it.*)

Ashby: She'll kill us. Meacher'll kill us if she finds out.

(*Ashby takes out the photo. He picks up a pair of scissors. Snips one of the pictures off.*)

Sergeant: Her photo, man. Don't, man. What you want that for? That's daft, that is.

Ashby: Read it in a book. These knights, they carried a picture of a girl round everywhere. If they died in a fight with a dragon or anything, it was the last thing they looked at before they died.

Sergeant: That's olden days, man.

Ashby: You don't understand anything, you don't.

Sergeant: Stupid Sandra Linaker. All she talks about is horses. Anyway, she's cross-eyed.

Ashby (*Grabs him*)**:** You what?

Sergeant: Only said she was cross-eyed, man.

Ashby: She's heck as like cross-eyed.

Sergeant: What you gonna do with it?

Ashby: Keep it. You have to keep it near your heart.

Sergeant: Stupid. You wait till I tell . . .

Ashby: Don't you tell anybody.

Sergeant: I wouldn't.

Ashby: We're blood brothers.

(*Ashby takes out the scissors.*)

Sergeant: Since when?

Ashby: Give us your thumb.

Sergeant: What you doing, man? Geroff me thumb, man.

Ashby: I'll do it first then.

(*Ashby cuts himself.*)

Sergeant: You cut yourself.

Ashby: Now you.

Sergeant: You get blood poisoning, man. You could die of that. If I die of blood poisoning, me mam'll kill us. It won't cut, Ashy. Got this hard skin. Some people have this hard skin and no matter how hard you cut . . .

Ashby: Let me . . . (*Ashby cuts Sergeant's thumb.*)

Sergeant: Ouch. That hurt.

Ashby: Press them together. Now we have to swear that we're blood brothers for ever and ever. If anyone does anything to me you have to revenge it; even unto death. And I do the same for you. Especially you don't say anything about me and Sandra Linaker. Swear over her picture. Swear.

Sergeant: I swear. Ashy, I feel faint, man.

Ashby: Someone coming.

(*Cropper enters with Trask.*)

Cropper: What you doing?

Sergeant: Only Cropper.

Cropper: What you doing in her desk?

Ashby: Nothing. I dropped my note.

Cropper: What note?

Ashby: Going to Cleveleys. We had to bring a note.

Cropper: Cleveleys? Trask.

Trask: What, Cropper?

Cropper: Clear off.

   (*Trask exits.*)

   Stupid school trip.

   (*He takes out a cigarette. Lights it.*)

Ashby: What's them, man?

Cropper: Gold Flake.

Sergeant: Gold Flake!

Cropper: They're the best. They taste like chocolate. Try it.

Sergeant: Meacher'll smell it.

Cropper: You scared, Sago?

Sergeant (*Nods*):   Course not. Dead strong, these.

Ashby: My dad smokes Woodbines.

Cropper: Rubbish, them.

Ashby: Not. They're dead strong.

Cropper: Not like these. Try it.

(*Smokes.*)

What you think?

Ashby: Yeah.

Cropper: Strong in't they?

Ashby: All right.

Cropper: Course they are. What you think o' the flavour?

Ashby: Well . . . kinda chocolate . . . you know.

Cropper: See. Give Sago a puff.

Sergeant: I got to go.

Cropper (*He grabs Sergeant.*): Inhale. (*Sergeant does so. Coughs.*) It's his first. Good, in't it?

Sergeant: Yeah. (*Cough*) Dead good.

Cropper (*To Ashby*): Got your ten bob?

(*Ashby takes out a ten-shilling note. And the letter. Cropper grabs them.*)

Now you haven't. Here, it isn't signed.

Ashby: It *is* signed.

Cropper: It's got to be signed by your mum and dad. Just your dad signed.

Ashby: My mum couldn't.

Cropper: Can't write her name.

Ashby: Shut up.

Cropper: Run off with the milkman.

Ashby: She was out. Give it us here.

Cropper: My dad showed me a new punch last night. It can kill you in ten seconds. Look, I'll show you, Sago.

Sergeant: Gerroff . . .

Cropper: Just like that. (*Cropper holds Sergeant and punches him on the arm.*)

Sergeant: Ouch. That hurt, man. Your dad's a boxer in't he, Cropper?

Cropper: North Eastern All Comers.

(*He shadow-boxes.*)

My cig's gone out. Light it with this.

(*Waves the ten shilling note.*)

Ashby: Don't mess about Croppy, man. It's a fake anyway.

Cropper: Where?

Ashby: It's got this mark on it. Here.

(*Cropper gives him the note and the letter.*)

Cropper: I wouldn't go to Cleveleys anyway. We went to Harrogate last year. Saw a dead dog on the beach.

Sergeant: Dexter's coming.

Cropper: Here, hold this.

(*He gives Ashby his cigarette.*)

Sergeant: Dexter's coming.

(*Ashby looks round. They're already on their way out.*)

Dexter: What are you boys doing in here at break?

Cropper: Just taking our work to Miss Meacher, sir.

Sergeant: We had work to finish, sir.

(*Sergeant and Cropper exit. Ashby in desperation puts the cigarette, the letter and the ten-bob note into his pocket.*)

Dexter: What about you, Ashby?

Ashby: Sir?

Dexter: What are you up to, boy?

Ashby: Not up to anything.

Dexter: Sir.

Ashby: Sir.

Dexter: Don't smile at me.

Ashby: Wasn't smiling, sir. I can't help it, I just look like it, sir.

Dexter: And don't sulk at me.

Ashby: I wasn't sulking, sir.

Dexter: Something going on. Don't think you can put one over on me. I can see through you lot, easy as winking. That's one thing the army taught me.

Ashby: Sir, is that true that you were a spy, sir?

Dexter: Not really a spy, Ashby. No, when Montgomery landed his forces in . . . Are you trying to be funny, Ashby?

Ashby: No, sir. Can I go now, sir?

Dexter: Take your hands out of your pockets.

Ashby: Sir, I . . . .

Dexter: Take them out. Slovenly boy. If you'd been in my platoon, I'd have taught you something. And stand still. What are you squirming about for?

Ashby: Nothing, sir.

Dexter: Well, stand still . . .

(*Sniffs.*)

What's that smell?

Ashby: Smell, sir?

Dexter: Something burning. Like paper smouldering.

Ashby: It's outside sir. Shall I go and have a look?

Dexter: It's those dustbins. Someone's set them on fire again. You wait till I get hold of . . .

(*He storms out. We hear his voice.*)

Get away from those dustbins. Now just stand still.

(*Whistle blows, off.*)

What have I said about those dustbins . . . .?

(*Ashby pulls out the cigarette and stamps it out. Then the letter and the ten shilling note. Both badly charred. He looks at them. Exits left.*
    Girls run on giggling. They form a circle round Sandra Linaker. They hold hands and skip round singing.)

All: Sandra Linaker, tell us true
       Where is the boy who will marry you?
       Is he handsome, is he tall?

Did you kiss him by the garden wall?
Where is the boy that you love best?
Is he North?

(*She shakes her head.*)

Or South?

(*Shakes her head.*)

Or East?

(*Likewise.*)

Or West?

Sandra: West.

(*She points. All run off screaming and giggling.*)

All: It's West.
I know who it is.
No. It isn't him.

(*Sandra and Phyllis are left alone. Phyllis starts doing handstands against the wall. Sandra gets out a small mirror and explores her face.*)

Phyllis: You know that Irene Ollerenshaw? Well, I hate her. Sandra. Sandra. She's spiteful.

Sandra: I think I'm getting freckles.

Phyllis: You know if you had to say who was your best friend, Sandra? Who would it be, Sandra? Who would it be?

Sandra: I read in this book. You rub them with lemon. Bits of lemon and they go away.

Phyllis: I saw you with Irene Ollerenshaw at dinner. You were sitting with her. She's not your best friend, is she, Sandra? She's not, is she, honest?

Sandra: I didn't sit with her. She sat with me. I'd never sit with Irene Ollerenshaw.

Phyllis: I saw her in the toilets, after swimming. Have I to tell you what she was doing?

Sandra: I don't want to know about Irene Ollerenshaw.

Phyllis: No, neither do I. Some people think she's the prettiest girl in the school. But I don't.

Sandra: Who thinks?

Phyllis: I don't think you can be pretty if you're common and smell.

(*Pause.*)

Sandra: You know what I do first thing in the morning?

Phyllis: What Sandra?

Sandra: I look at myself in the mirror. Look at my face. I give myself points out of ten. I say: nose, seven; eyes, eight; lips, nine-and-a-half.

Phyllis: You've got the best lips in school, Sandra.

Sandra: Sometimes I give high marks. Sometimes I give low. Yesterday I got seventy-nine out of a hundred.

Phyllis: Seventy-nine, Sandra. Gosh! Nobody else gets seventy-nine.

Sandra: Sometimes I'm too critical.

Phyllis: Yeah, so am I.

Sandra: When my freckles go, I'll get ninety. I'm aiming for ninety.

Phyllis: Ninety. Nobody in the world gets ninety. (*Pause.*) Sandra?
You know, what d'you think I'd get?

Sandra: Forty.

Phyllis: Forty! Only forty.

Sandra: Forty's good. If you've got glasses and you're a bit fat.

Phyllis: Well, yeah. (*Pause.*) My mum says I've got pretty hair.

Sandra: They're all coming back. I'm going the lavvy.

Phyllis: Shall I come with you, Sandra?

Sandra: No.

(*Sandra exits, right.*
We hear the sound of the girls getting closer, then rushing past, but we don't see them. Meanwhile Phyllis looks at her face in the mirror. She wrinkles her nose. She takes off her glasses. Puts her face sideways, gives a smile.
Sergeant has entered, left. Phyllis realises Sergeant is watching her.)

Phyllis: You'll know me next time.

Sergeant: Wouldn't want to.

Phyllis: Ha! Ha!

Sergeant: You'll crack it.

Phyllis: What you staring at?

Sergeant: A pig and its breakfast.

Phyllis: You should know — oink, oink.

Sergeant: You seen Eric Ashby?

Phyllis: Wouldn't want to.

Sergeant: Blood brothers. Me and Eric. We fight for each other to the death.

Phyllis: Stupid.
Look, there's Miss Meacher showing her knickers.

(*Sergeant looks round.*)

>   Made you look, I made you stare,
>   Made the barber cut your hair.

(*Morpeth runs past them and exits. He is followed shortly after by Trask and Cropper chasing him and shouting.*)

Phyllis: What's Jacky Cropper and them chasing him for?

Sergeant: Always bashing somebody.

Phyllis: Only cos he's bigger.

Sergeant: Know this one? This pudding goes into a sweet shop with a dead cat and . . .

Phyllis: Heard it. You should be on the stage.

Sergeant: Yeah?

Phyllis: It's just leaving town.

Sergeant: Smell cheese.

Phyllis: Gerroff, I know it.

Sergeant: Where's Sandra Linaker?

Phyllis: Gone the lavvy. Why would you want to know where she is?

Sergeant: Nothing.

(*Morpeth runs past with Trask and Cropper chasing as before. Pause.*)

Sergeant: Bet you I know something you don't know.

Phyllis: If you know it, it's not worth knowing.

Sergeant: Won't tell you then.

Phyllis: See if I care. Anyway I know something you don't know.

Sergeant: Just saying that. You know Dexter?

Phyllis: Yeah.

Sergeant: Well, you know his leg. It's wooden.

Phyllis: How d'you know?

Sergeant: Eric Ashby crawled under his desk and stuck a pin in it and he didn't jump. He said he was injured in the war.

Phyllis: He was.

Sergeant: Never. He caught it in a bus door.

Phyllis: Who said? You fib!

Sergeant: Me dad says so. He saw him.

Phyllis: That what you wanted to tell me?

Sergeant: Course not.

Phyllis: If it's about Sandra Linaker and this lad. I know it.

Sergeant: How did you know?

Phyllis: Wouldn't you like to know. He told me.

Sergeant: Ashby told *you*.

Phyllis: No but you have. Ah ha!

Sergeant: You . . .

(*Pause.*)

Phyllis: Might as well tell me the rest now.

Sergeant: You tell me yours.

Phyllis: You first. He wants to go out with her. Ashby does. He does, doesn't he?

Sergeant: Yeah.

Phyllis: I knew it anyway.

Sergeant: Don't tell her.

Phyllis: Think I'm a tell-tale tit.

Sergeant: Don't tell *anybody*.

Phyllis: Course not.

Sergeant: Tell us yours now.

Phyllis: I wouldn't tell you.

Sergeant: I told you mine.

Phyllis: That's why I'm not telling. You can't keep a secret. T.T.F.N.

Sergeant: Promise not to tell.

Phyllis: Course. Cross me heart.

(*She gets up. Irene and Denise walk across arm-in-arm. Phyllis joins them.*)

Phyllis: Bet I know something you don't . . .

Denise:⎫
⎬ What?
Irene:⎭

Phyllis: You know Eric Ashby? Well, you know Sandra Linaker? You'll never guess what Sago just told us . . .

(*They exit right, whispering, giggling and swapping astonished gasps.*
    Trask and Cropper rush on. They stop, obviously looking round for Morpeth. Their eyes light on Sergeant.)

Cropper: You seen Morpeth?

Sergeant: What you want him for?

Cropper: Just to bash him up. What you talking to her for?

Sergeant: Who?

Cropper: Big Bottom.

Sergeant: Nothing.

Cropper: Talking about me, were you?

Sergeant: Course not, Croppy, man. (*He sidles.*)

Cropper: Where you goin'?

Sergeant: I was just, er . . . you know . . .

Cropper: You come here. Didn't say you could go, did I?

Sergeant: No.

Cropper: Remember when we hung you out the second floor window?

Trask: Yeah, by his ankles.

Cropper: Good that.

Trask: Didn't half scream . . . (*Grabs Sergeant.*)

Cropper: What about Ashby?

Sergeant: What about him?

Cropper: You was going through desks.

Sergeant: Wasn't.

Cropper: Course you was. (*Thumps Sergeant casually on the upper arm.*) Wasn't you?

Sergeant: We was looking, yeah.

Cropper: What for? He took something. What was it?

Sergeant: Nothing.

Cropper: My Dad showed me this other punch. Break your arm he said. Stick your knuckle out. Course you have to do it hard. (*He thumps Sergeant.*) What was it?

Sergeant: Nothing. Didn't take nothing.

Cropper: Are you sure? Here, hold him, Trask.

(*Trask pinions Sergeant's arms from behind.*)

What was it?

Sergeant: Gerroff, man. Give over hitting me.

Cropper: What was it? Unless you want to get hit.

Sergeant: It was . . . nothing, man. Nothing.

(*Cropper thumps him hard.*)

Sergeant: Ouch. That hurt, man.

(*Cropper punches him again.*)

Give over, Cropper.

Trask: Cropper, there's Morpy. (*Lets go of Sergeant.*)

Cropper: Let you off this time.

(*They walk away, right. Just before they exit, Sergeant shouts.*)

Sergeant: Ah you. You're nothing, Crophead. Smelly bum!

(*They turn.*)

Couldn't knock the skin off a rice pudding!

(*Sergeant runs off left with Cropper and Trask chasing. They nearly knock over Sandra and Phyllis who enter left, arm-in-arm.*)

Sandra: Stupid lads. Always fighting. I'd never go out with a boy from this school.

Phyllis: Nor me. (*Pause.*) Sandra?

Sandra: What?

Phyllis: Am I your best friend?

Sandra: Wish there were lads like in this story I'm reading.

Phyllis: Am I, Sandra? Am I your best friend?

Sandra: Phyllis? What d'you think of me? You know my looks.

Phyllis: Well . . . think you're ever so pretty, Sandra. Honest.

Sandra: Only pretty. Not . . . beautiful.

Phyllis: What's the difference?

Sandra: Beautiful is . . . more serious. If you're beautiful, in the end men will die because they're in love with you.

Phyllis: I think you're beautiful, Sandra.

Sandra: Yes, I know.

Phyllis: Who would you like to die for you?

Sandra: Don't know. I haven't made up my mind.

(*Sergeant, chased by Cropper and Trask, crosses left to right.*)

Phyllis: I know somebody who would.

Sandra: Who?

Phyllis: I'm not supposed to tell.

Sandra: I thought you wanted to be my best friend.

Phyllis: It's a secret.

Sandra: If you don't tell me, Phyllis Sidebotham, I'll never speak to you again.

(*Pause.*)

Phyllis: Eric Ashby.

Sandra: Eric Ashby.

Phyllis: Sago said to tell you that he told him that I was to tell you if you wanted to go out with him.

Sandra: I wouldn't go out with Eric Ashby.

Phyllis: No. Neither would I. You won't say I said, will you?

Sandra: I won't tell. (*Pause.*) Phyllis?

Phyllis: Yeah. Sandra?

Sandra: You're my best friend.

(*Lights fade to blackout.*)

All: Mr Dexter is our teacher
Teaches English, Art and sums
If we get our answers wrong
He canes us on our bums.
He says he is an army hero
Lost his leg in the war
But we know he only caught it
In the lavatory door.

(*Noise of a classroom. Conversation. Chairs scraping.*)

Dexter: All right. Simmer down, Class 4.
(*Lights up on a classroom scene. Seats at an angle. A blackboard. Mr Dexter addressing the class.*)

Simmer down. Now, there's the date on the board. And there's the title. What I Would Like To Be When I Grow Up.

Trask: Sir my nib's broke, sir.

Dexter: Capitals for the title. Date in the top right-hand corner and don't forget, start a half-inch in from the margin.

Trask: Sir, my nib's broke, sir.

Dexter: One day your neck will be broken and it will be me who's done it, Trask.

Trask: It's broke sir. I've done all blots.

Sergeant: Sir, I can't find my Composition book, sir.

Dexter: You'd lose your head if it was loose, Sergeant lad. Use your rough book.

Now, I want you to imagine yourself some time in the future. Tell me all about it in your best handwriting.

Morpeth: How d'you spell 'appendicitis' sir?

Dexter: What are you writing about, Morpeth?

Morpeth: An operation, sir. I'm going to be a surgeon.

Dexter: Good, get on with it.

Morpeth: You haven't told me how you spell it, sir.

Dexter: Spell what?

Morpeth: Appendicitis.

Dexter: You've got a dictionary, Morpeth?

Morpeth: Yes, sir.

Dexter: Well use it, lad, use it, that's what it's there for.

Sergeant: Sir, you collected in the rough books.

Dexter: What?

Sergeant: You collected them in, sir, the rough books.

Dexter: Well, get some paper.

Ashby: Sir, could you imagine you're anything, sir?

Dexter: I should think so.

Ashby: Could you imagine you was a soldier, sir?

Dexter: I don't see why not.

Ashby: It was just that I was thinking, sir, about how you told us about your adventures in the war, sir. Abroad, sir.

Dexter: Found that interesting did you?

Ashby: Yes, sir.

Cropper: Really exciting, sir.

Sergeant: Tell us again, sir.

Dexter: That'll do. What exactly did you want to know, Ashby?

Ashby: About the way those natives could kill one another by just thinking about it and saying their name. I mean, could anybody do it, sir?

Sergeant (*Sotto voce*): I'd kill Meacher.

Cropper: I'd kill you.

Ashby: It was dead interesting, sir.

Dexter: That was ... erm ... in Burma. Of course, not everyone could do it. They had to have this power, d'you see. Well they said the name of their victim and, well, he would fall sick or have a headache or sometimes, even, eventually die.

Ashby: Did you do it, sir?

Phyllis: Whose name did you say?

Trask: Could you do it now, sir?

Dexter: Of course not, Trask.

Trask (*Pretending to die*): Ah, he did it. I'm dying.

Ashby: Is that when you got your wound, sir?

Dexter: Oh that. No, that was in Italy. We'd been ordered by HQ to attack this redoubt ...

Morpeth: HQ stands for Headquarters doesn't it, sir?

Dexter: That's right, Morpeth. It was a pocket of resistance in the hills. I got my platoon together and I told them straight: 'Look here, chaps this could be pretty dicey.' Well, we set out . . .

(*He suddenly realises that there is silence and all the class are leaning on their elbows, staring at him.*)

Now come on, get on with that writing. Trask, you haven't even started.

Trask: My nib's crossed.

Dexter: Get another one.

Trask: I've looked, sir. There aren't any.

Dexter: Well, use a pencil. And you can stay in over break and copy it out properly.

Trask: Sir, I haven't got a pencil.

Dexter: Use this one. (*Gives him a propelling pencil.*)

Irene: What's the title, sir?

Dexter: Do you have eyes, Irene Ollerenshaw?

Irene: Yes, sir.

Dexter: Well, use them. It's on the board.

Irene: Sir, it's shining, sir.

Dexter: Come and sit over here.

Phyllis: She's not sitting there. That's my place.

Dexter: For goodness' sake.

Phyllis: Sir, Irene Ollerenshaw's sitting in my place, sir.

Dexter: Sit here, Irene. Now settle down. I want this story finished by break . . .

Trask: Sir?

Dexter: Or you'll be in finishing it in your own time . . .

Trask: Sir?

Dexter: And if it's not finished by then you'll be in at dinner time.

Trask: Sir?

Dexter: What is it now?

Trask: Sir, there's no lead in this pencil.

Ashby: He's broke it, sir.

Morpeth: It's a Parker. They cost pounds.

Irene: Aw, he's broke sir's pencil.

Dexter: Be quiet. Out here, Trask.

Trask: What for, sir?

Dexter: You can finish it at break and dinner time and tomorrow.

Trask: What have I done, sir?

Dexter: Out here.

Trask: That's not fair, sir.

Dexter: OUT! Face the wall. LOOK, NOW GET ON WITH YOUR WORK. SERGEANT, YOU HAVEN'T WRITTEN ONE WORD. GET OUT! GET OUT! GET OUTSIDE!

Sergeant: Sir.

Dexter: OUTSIDE!

(*Sergeant goes out. Dexter throws Sergeant's book after him.*)

TAKE YOUR BOOK WITH YOU!

(*With excessive and deliberate calm.*)

Now, the rest of you. Work.

Phyllis: Sir?

Dexter: Yes, Phyllis?

Phyllis: What do we have to write about?

Dexter: RIGHT. Put down your pens. All of you. Ashby, put your pen down. All eyes on the board. What does it say? It says the date. Read it.

All: March 15th 1948.

Dexter: LOUDER.

All: MARCH 15TH 1948.

Dexter: Do you understand that Phyllis? That's called the date. Now, the title.

All: WHAT I WOULD LIKE TO BE WHEN I GROW UP.

Dexter: Wonderful. Now write down the date. Write down the title and underneath write your composition. And let's not have another sound until the bell goes. Now, lift up your pens. And write.

Ashby: Sir?

Dexter: WRITE!

(*All heads are down. Cowed. In the following, each head comes up looking into the far distance almost in a trance. It should be clear that they are speaking their dreams aloud.*)

Sandra: Sandra Linaker; Composition. March 15th 1948. What I Would Like To Be When I Grow Up. When I grow up, my ambition is to own a white horse and become the first girl to ride for England. I would have a house with flowers and a whip and a soda syphon on the table and there would be cups and rosettes everywhere.

Phyllis: My best ambition is to be a stable girl. In the mornings I would put a saddle on Sandra's horse and wash it and make sure everything was clean and shiny.

Cropper: I am a boxer. I wear big gloves and shorts. I have my name on the back of my silk dressing gown. It says Kid Cropper. I punch them till they are knocked out cold. I walk into Madison Square Gardens to fight Joe Louis for the heavyweight championship of the world. The crowd call out my name.

All (*With heads down and in a hoarse whisper*): CROPPER-CROPPER-CROPPER.

(*Cropper rises looking into the faraway. He raises both hands in the air in victory. They cheer softly and distantly.*)

Aaaaaaaaaaaaaaaaaaah.

(*As Cropper sinks to his desk, Ashby's head comes up.*)

Ashby: Dear Sandra.
You don't know who I am but I love you. Please don't tell anybody about this. It is a secret.

Sandra: The England trainer's eyes twinkled in his
weatherbeaten face as he smiled at Sandra.
'It's up to you now my girl.'
Sandra nodded nervously but there was determination in
her pretty blue eyes. 'You know what you have to do. It just
needs a clear round out there in front of that fifty thousand
crowd and the Germans will be beaten and the cup will be
ours.'

Phyllis: Phyllis, her stablemaid and best friend, tightened up
the girth of Sportsman. She was a plain girl but had a good
heart and pretty hair.

Dexter: Corporal Dexter felt the sword touch his shoulder.
His expression was modest but the King knew that there was
endurance and an iron will there. The King spoke softly:
'Arise, Sir Anthony Vincent Dexter, VC and Knight.'

(*Dexter rises slowly. The rest of the class clap softly under their
desks.*)

Ashby: I think about you all the time and I wrote your initials
on my ruler. If you like me a lot . . . If you like me I can
walk home your way past the Institute and the Co-op. Or
you could ride back on my handlebars. I could also see you
behind the bike sheds in the girls' playground on Thursday
after school dinners. Signed: An Admirer.
PS If you don't want to see me don't tell anybody else if you
think you know who I am or someone has told you.
PPS If you do come don't bring anybody else. PPPS Don't
show this letter to nobody.

(*Denise enters.*)

Dexter: Yes, Denise?
Get on with your work. Just because someone comes in the room, that isn't a general invitation for you to put your pens down.

Denise: Sir, Miss Meacher said to remind you to collect the money and the signed letters about going to Cleveleys on the school trip and can she have them right away.

Dexter: Can? What does she want right away?

Denise: The letters sir.

Dexter: After . . .

Denise: *Can* she have the letters?

Dexter: Can?

Denise: *May* she have the letters?

Dexter: That's better.

Irene: Sir, can I collect them?

Trask: Sir, can I sir?

Cropper: I'm not going.

Irene: Please, sir.

Dexter: Hands down.

Phyllis: Sir, I've brought mine.

Dexter: Hands down.

Trask: Sir. Me, sir.

Dexter: SHUT UP!
Now I've just about had enough of you for today Class 4.

Now we can do this properly in a civilised manner or we can
wait here all day until I get proper behaviour. Which is it to
be? We can wait here until five o'clock if you like. It's your
time you're wasting you know, not mine.

  Right. Now, if you're going to Cleveleys a week on
Thursday and you've got your ten-shilling notes and your
signed letters bring them out in alphabetical order.

  Ashby.

(*Ashby dreams of Sandra. He writes his letter.*)

ASHBY!

Cropper: He's asleep, sir.

Dexter: What are you writing?

Ashby: Sir?

Dexter: I told you to stop writing. Bring it here.

(*Ashby slides the letter under his pad.*)

Come here.

(*Ashby walks to the front with his book.*)

What 's this supposed to be?

Ashby: Composition sir.

Dexter: Composition . There's nothing here. What have you
  been doing for the last twenty minutes?

Ashby: Nothing, sir.

Dexter: I can see that, Ashby. You don't have to tell me
  that. You've been wasting your time again, haven't you?

Ashby: Been thinking, sir.

Dexter: What with?

(*He hurls the book to the back of the class.*)

That's an insult, Ashby.

(*Ashby goes to retrieve the book.*)

Where d'you think you're going?
    I didn't say you could go. Did I say you could go?

Ashby: No sir.

Dexter: No, sir. Ashby you're a lazy, stupid little layabout.
What are you?

Ashby: Lazy, stupid little layabout, sir.

Dexter: Mmh. Where is it?

Ashby: Where's what, sir?

Dexter: The letter, you dunderhead.

Ashby: What letter? I wasn't writing a letter.

Dexter: Who said anything about writing a letter?

Ashby: Sir, I thought . . .

Dexter: You know what thought did don't you, Ashby?

All: Followed a dust cart . . .

Dexter: That'll do.
The letter, lad. The letter from your mother and father and
your ten-shilling note. You are going, aren't you?

Ashby: Yes, sir.
(*Pause.*)

Dexter: Well?

Ashby: Yes, sir.

Dexter: Then hand it over.

Ashby: I can't, sir.

Dexter: Where is it? I suppose you've left it at home.

Ashby: No, sir.

Dexter: Where is it?

Ashby: Pocket, sir.

Dexter: Then give it to me . . .

Ashby: I can't, sir.

Dexter: Give it to me!

(*Ashby takes out the charred debris and puts it in Dexter's extended palm.*)
What's this?

Ashby: Letter, sir.

(*Dexter looks.*)

And that's the ten bob, sir.

Cropper: Pants caught fire, sir.

Dexter: Cut the cackle, Cropper. How did this happen, Ashby?

Ashby: I don't know, sir.

Dexter: Don't give me that, boy. Don't give me that. A letter and a ten-shilling note catch fire in your pocket and you don't know why. D'you take me for a fool, Ashby?

(*Ashby has noticed that Cropper has found his letter and is making it into a dart. He makes a surreptitious gesture with his fist.*)

Well? Ashby, I'm talking to you.

(*Dexter turns away towards Sergeant.*)

You can come in. Sit down and behave yourself.

(*During this, Ashby is threatening Cropper with gestures and whispers threateningly.*
    Cropper hurls the dart into the air. Dexter returns. The dart floats through the air in wide circles. Dexter stops short and watches it. It lands. Dexter picks it up.)

Dexter: Who threw this? WHO THREW THIS?

Ashby: Shall I put it in the basket for you, sir?

Dexter: WHO THREW THIS DART? (*Silence.*) I can wait all day. (*Silence.*) Very well.

(*He opens it and reads. Ashby raises a fist at Cropper.*)

This is a letter. What boy wrote this letter? It is a letter from a boy in this class. It is a disgusting letter. I will not have this sort of behaviour going on in my class.
    Sandra Linaker. Do you know anything about this letter?

Sandra (*Stands*): No, sir.

Dexter: Have you any idea who wrote it?

Sandra: No, sir.

Dexter: Very well. You may sit down. (*She sits.*)
    Sandra tells me she knows nothing of this letter and I believe her. Now. I'm bitterly disappointed. I don't mind

boys helping girls with their satchels or carrying their bags
for them or making sure they cross the street safely or open
the doors for them. That is proper behaviour. That is
gentlemanly behaviour. But I will not have this kind of
sneaky, underhand thing. It leads to all sorts of things that
aren't . . . gentlemanly. And I will not have it going on in
my class. D'you hear, will not. I'm giving you one more
chance. It's no good protecting each other. I shall find out
even if I have to send every boy in the class for the cane.

Sergeant: It came from over there, sir.

Dexter: Near Cropper?

Sergeant: I was watching through the window, sir.

Dexter: Cropper. What do you know about this?

Cropper: I never wrote it, sir.

Dexter: It's all over your face, Cropper. Guilt.is all over your
face.

Cropper: I didn't . . .

Dexter: Did you throw it?

Cropper: I threw it, sir, but . . . .

Dexter: Ah ha!

Cropper: But it was Ashby who . . . . .

Dexter: Ashby?

Ashby: I never threw it, sir. How could I throw it, sir? I was
out here.

Irene: Ashby never threw it, sir. I'd have seen.

Dexter: You know nothing about this letter, Ashby? Well?

Ashby: No, sir.

(*The bell rings.*)

Dexter: I'll get to the bottom of this dirty business. Cropper go and stand outside the staffroom. If you think this is going to stop here, you're very much mistaken. The rest of you, dismiss.

(*They file out whispering. Dexter pushes past the last two, Sandra and Phyllis. Sandra waits then goes back. She picks up the letter. She sees Phyllis watching her. Reads the letter. The lights fade on her .... to blackout.*
    In the blackout the sound of a skipping rope. We hear Ashby's voice whispering but clearly audible.)

Ashby: Don't look down. Whatever you do, don't look down. Five hundred feet. One false move and it's certain death on the rocks below.

(*During the speech a spotlight on Ashby's face, left.*
The spot widens to show him on his bike, his eyes closed, arms outstretched, balanced and still. Centre is Phyllis skipping. She mouths the numbers in a whisper.)

Phyllis: Ninety-four, 'nty five, 'ty six .... (etc.)....

Ashby: And he stops. The crowd watch him. He wobbles. Is he going to fall? No. The crowd roars, Aaaaaaah.

Phyllis: What you doing?

Ashby: Cycling.

Phyllis: Hundred 'n one, 'dred and two ...

Ashby: Blindfold over Niagara.

Phyllis: Niwhosalump?

Ashby: Niagara.

Phyllis: We had one but the back wheel came off.

Ashby: If you close your eyes it could be. It's the same; all those people like ants.

Phyllis: You're dead stupid you are, Eric Ashby.

Ashby: You don't have to look down or you get scared. It's only being scared makes you fall.

Phyllis: Daft. He's daft as a brush, isn't he, Sandra?

(*Sandra sits, right, reading.*)

Dred'n fifteen ... (*etc.*) ...
  Where d'you pinch your bike?

Ashby: Mine.

Phyllis: Like the coalman said when he fell down the hole.

Ashby: Mum bought it. For me birthday.

Phyllis: Raleigh; useless them.

Ashby: Heck as like. They're the best. Dad said so.

Phyllis: Anyway, you're not supposed to be here. You're not supposed to be in the girls' playground.

Ashby: Who says?

Phyllis: Miss Meacher says. Didn't she, Sandra?

Ashby: Yeah well, she's not here, is she?

Phyllis: Soon will be if I tell her.

Ashby: Like to see you.

Phyllis: Well, I will. Tell her about the letter and all.

Ashby: What letter?

Phyllis: Ah ha. That'd be telling.

Ashby: Don't know what you're talking about.

Phyllis: Have I to ask him, Sandra?

Ashby: The letter Dexter found.

(*Phyllis walks over from Sandra to Ashby again.*)

Phyllis: That letter Cropper threw in class. You want to go out with her don't you? Have I to ask her? She won't, but I'll ask her. Have I to?

(*Sound of shouting and screaming off.*)

Phyllis: Eric Ashby wants to know if . . . What's that row?

(*She runs past Sandra and stares out right, but still in sight.*)

Eh, there's a fight. There's a fight, Sandra. It's Jacky Cropper and Sergeant.

Ashby: Sergeant?

Phyllis: Cropper's murdering him. I'm going. You coming? I'm going.

(*She runs off right.*)

Sandra: Stupid lads fighting.

(*Ashby cycles round in a circle. Sandra sits once more.*)

Ashby: If I said I did, would you? If I said I wrote it, would you?

Sandra: If you said you wrote what, would I what?

Ashby: You know.

Sandra: I don't know. No.

Ashby: Like — I could go home your way.

Sandra: It's miles. Other side of the Moss.

Ashby: Not far. Would you, eh? Would you?

Sandra: I might . . .

Ashby: Honest?

Sandra: And I might not. That why you came?

Ashby: What?

Sandra: See if I was here.

Ashby: Dunno. Might have done.

Sandra: D'you think I'm pretty?

Ashby: Yeah, all right.

Sandra: Only all right.

Ashby: Yeah . . . you know, all right.

Sandra: What you like best?

Ashby: What you mean, best?

Sandra: Like which d'you think is my best feature? Hair?
Eyes? What d'you think's best?

Ashby: I don't know.

Sandra: Go on, say. I won't tell.

Ashby: Dunno . . . It's just that . . . dunno.

Sandra: But you like me, don't you?

Ashby: All right.

Sandra: How much? Just all right or a lot?

Ashby: Mh?

Sandra: A lot?

Ashby: Yeah.

Sandra: A lot?

Ashby: Yeah you know . . . a lot.

Sandra: I knew you did.

Ashby: How you know?

Sandra: Seen you looking. That time when we were tracing maps of the Red Sea. That's why you come. See if I was here. That's what it said in the letter.

Ashby: You read my letter?

Sandra: See! I knew you wrote it. Else you wouldn't have said *my* letter.

Ashby: I heard it when Dexter read it out. That's how I knew.

Sandra: He didn't read it.

(*Pause.*)

Ashby: I was only messing about.

Sandra: Didn't you mean it, then?

Ashby: Mean what?

Sandra: About being in love.

Ashby: Might have done. (*Pause.*) Well?

Sandra: Well. Two wells make a hole and you fell in it. With your head well in it.

Ashby: Like after school. You want to?

Sandra: What?

Ashby: Walk home with us.

(*Pause.*)

Sandra: What you think of Irene Ollerenshaw?

Ashby: Irene Ollerenshaw? All right.

Sandra: Think she's more pretty than me?

Ashby: No.

Sandra: She'll go out with you.

Ashby: With me?

Sandra: She likes you. She told me. She'll go out with you.

Ashby: Irene Ollerenshaw?

Sandra: She'll go out with anybody.

Phyllis (*Runs on from right***):** Sago and Jacky Cropper had a fight. Sago's nose is bleeding.

(*Sergeant runs on crying. Blood from his nose. His jacket torn.*)

Sergeant: Ashy. It's Jacky Cropper, man. He hit me, man. Stop him, Ashy.

(*Cropper enters right, followed by Trask, Irene, Morpeth and others. Sergeant is separated from Ashby. Cropper advances with Trask.*)

Cropper: You had enough, Sago?

Sergeant: Stop him, Ashy.

Cropper: You want more?

Sergeant: Don't you hit me again. Ashy'll get you. Won't you, Ashy? Ashy. Blood brothers, Ashy. Remember?

Cropper: You going to stop me, Ashby? Remember what happened last time?

(*Pause. Trask grabs Sergeant. Cropper thumps Sergeant.*)

Don't do it again. Don't ever tell on me again.

Sergeant: Ashy.

Cropper: Understand? Understand?

Sergeant: Yeah.

Cropper: Mates?

(*Cropper holds out his hand. Sergeant shakes it.*)

Sergeant (*Turns on Ashby*): It was him. It was him took that photo. I saw him. He cut it out.

Sandra: My picture?

Sergeant: It was him. I wouldn't say before.

Ashby: Shut up, you.

(*Ashby goes for Sergeant but Cropper steps in between.*)

Cropper: Don't you touch him. He's my mate now. Aren't you Sago?

Sergeant: I'm with you Jacky, lad.

(*Dexter enters right.*)

Dexter: What's all this?

(*They all back away, looking innocent but hovering curiously.*)

Who's been fighting? Cropper?

Cropper: Fighting, sir? Not me, sir.

Dexter: Sergeant. There's blood on your face.

Cropper: He fell over, sir. He was chasing a ball, sir and fell over against the wall.

Dexter: Is that right, Sergeant? (*Pause.*) Well?

Sergeant: Fell into a wall, sir.

Dexter: I see. Well, you know my rules about fighting. There's only one way to settle it and that's in the ring after school with the gloves on. By the rules. Like gentlemen. Not in the playground like savages.

All: Yes, sir.

Dexter: Just remember that. Now out of the girls' playground. You shouldn't be here anyway. Off you go.

(*Dexter exits.*)

Sandra: Where's my photo? You took my photo.

Ashby: What photo?

Cropper: Give it back, Ashby.

Ashby: No.

Cropper: Give it back.

Sergeant: It's in his top pocket.

Cropper: Give it to him.

(*Sergeant walks slowly across. Stands in front of Ashby.*)

Give it to him.

(*Ashby slowly takes the photo out and gives it to Sergeant. Sergeant gives it to Cropper. Cropper gives it to Sandra, and moves away. Pause.*)

You coming, Sago?

(*Pause. Then Sergeant walks towards Cropper and Trask and they exit, right. Ashby watches them. The others drift off, leaving Irene and Ashby. She has been eating an apple.*)

Irene: Have a go on your bike?

(*He nods. He extends his arms and begins to tightrope slowly.*)

What you doing?

Ashby: Walking. Across Niagara.

Irene: I do that.

(*She puts the bike down and begins to tightrope also.*)

Makes me dead nervous.

Ashby: Five hundred feet up.

Irene: She going out with him?

Ashby: Who?

Irene: Jacky Cropper and Sandra Linaker.

Ashby: Dunno.

Irene: Want my core?

(*Their hands are outstretched. He takes the core without looking and continuing to balance, takes a bite.*)

Ashby: Look at the people.

Irene: Yeah, like ants.

Ashby: Like pygmies.

Irene: Yeah. Don't look down.

Ashby: Can't help it. Someone waving.

Irene: Where? Yeah, I see.

Ashby: It's my mum. See my mum down there? They shouldn't wave — puts you off.

Irene: Yeah, puts you off.

Ashby: Can't see her now.

(*He makes a crashing sound. Falls.*)

Irene: What was that?

Ashby: I fell off.

Irene: Me too. I fell off.

(*Falls.*
   Sound of distant singing: 'Onward Christian Soldiers'. The lights fade. The singing becomes stronger. In the blackout the children line up at an angle for assembly. They should be so disposed that children and audience become the assembly but the audience must be able to see the children as well. Miss Meacher is pounding the piano, singing gustily and conducting.)

All: . . . With the cross of Jesus
Going on befooooooooore.

(*As the lights go up, we see Ashby and Irene Ollerenshaw stealthily creeping in and joining their class.*)

Meacher (*Without taking her eyes off the music*): If you think I haven't seen you creeping in late, you've got another think coming.

(*She pounds the introduction.*)

Last verse now. Shoulders back. Christian soldiers we're supposed to be, not meek little mice. Shoulders back, heads up.

FORWARD INTO BATTLE-ONE-TWO-THREE-FOUR
. . . .

(*School sings the last verse while Cropper, Ashby, Trask and Sergeant sing as follows.*)

All: Meacher our Headteacher
Always plays wrong notes,
Face is like a bus crash
Feet as big as boats,
She takes her wig off every night
Head's bald as an egg
One glass eye and big false teeth
And wears a wooden leg.

Meacher: There's a groaner.

All: Onward Christian soldiers . . .

(*She walks through the lines head cocked, listening. They part before her.*)

Marching as to war . . . . .

Meacher: Where's the fog horn?

All: With the cross of Jesus . . .

(*She slaps Trask across the head. It sends him staggering. The crack rings out. She doesn't pause in her step but is back at the lectern conducting.*)

Going on before.
AAAAAMEEEEEEN.

(*Pause.*)

Meacher: May the love of God
The goodness of Christ
Morpeth are you chewing? In the basket
And the charity of the Holy Spirit
Be with us now and for evermore.
Amen.

(*The children mumble along but her voice rises above. There is much coughing and shuffling.*)

Meacher: Stand still! Morpeth, you stay there 'til I tell you to go. Do you think God has nothing better to do than listen to your coughing this morning?
   Goodness me.

(*A child, out of sight, crashes to the floor in a faint. Dexter swoops in and bears her off in his arms. He returns later.*)

There's no need to look round. If she'd had a proper breakfast this morning she wouldn't have fainted.
   The netball team result.
Mary Street, 10. St Vincent de Paul's, 35.
   The Nurse is coming today so you'll bring your classes outside my room when you're called. I hope we're not going to have any dirty heads this term.
   Winner of this week's tidy desk competition.
Sandra Linaker, Class 4. Sandra, come and get your house points for Florence Nightingale House.
Yes, and where's the applause?

(*Clapping*)

Yes. I should think so.

Well, that's my pleasant duty. You know, I like to make assembly a happy time. We all like to be in a happy frame of mind at Mary Street when we start the day, don't we? Well don't we?

All: Yes, Miss Meacher.

Meacher: Of course we do. But you know there are always certain individuals who have to spoil it for the rest of us.

When I looked at my letters this morning there was a big envelope waiting for me. Well, I opened that letter and inside it was a photograph. But it wasn't an ordinary photograph. It was a special photograph. Can you guess what it was? It was the school . . .

All: Photograph.

Meacher: School photograph, that's right.

Morpeth: Miss, can I be excused?

Meacher: No, you can't. Why didn't you go before assembly?

Well, I looked at that photograph. Everybody smiling as if to say, 'I'm happy and proud to be a pupil at Mary Street Junior School,' they seemed to say.

Except, one. One, who wasn't smiling. One boy who moved. One boy who spoiled the whole photograph.

Jacky Cropper.

Out here.

(*Cropper walks out to the front.*)

Cropper: Miss, it wasn't me.

Meacher: It never is, is it? It's always somebody else. It's my

fault. Or Mr Dexter's. But never yours. It's never Jacky
Cropper's fault.

Cropper: Miss, it wasn't my fault.

Meacher: Look! Look here! The photograph. Everybody is
still. Everybody smiling. Everybody with their arms folded.
Except for Jacky Cropper. He's waving his arms and jumping
up and down.

(*Trask sniggers.*)

I don't think it's a laughing matter. Do you think it's a joke,
Peter Trask? Because if you do, I certainly don't.

Have you any idea, Jacky Cropper, what it cost to have
this photograph taken? Have you any idea what trouble I
went to? But of course, that doesn't matter to you, does it?
You think the whole world's there just for your benefit.

Cropper: Miss, I was pushed.

Meacher: I see, you were pushed now.

Cropper: Miss, I was. It was . . .

Meacher: Silence. I will not have tale-carriers in this school.
You're in enough trouble as it is. Already you've been sent to
me for writing letters to girls. Who thinks this is a joke?
Anybody who thinks it funny come out here and he can
explain the joke to me.

Do you think girls want to get letters from boys who move
about in the school photograph?

Cropper: Miss, that wasn't me, either.

Meacher: The same old story. Somebody else. You're in the
fourth year now Jacky Cropper. You should be setting an
example.

In this world some people go up, and some go down.
Young Cropper, you're going up. Go up to my room and wait
for me.

Mr Dexter, I want the punishment book.

(*Cropper goes down the room.*)

Cropper (*As he goes past Ashby*):   You wait, Ashby.

Meacher: The rest of you dismiss. Quietly!

Morpeth (*Still wriggling*):   Miss?

(*Meacher consults Dexter. The school files out. Ashby, Sandra
and Phyllis remain.*)

Phyllis: You're a fib, Eric Ashby.

Sandra: And yellow.

Phyllis: It was you pushed him.

Sandra: I saw.

Phyllis: So did I. If it was me, I'd tell.

Sandra: He'll get caned now.

Phyllis: And the letter.

Sandra: All your fault.

Phyllis: Think Sandra'd go out with someone like you? You
wouldn't, would you, Sandra?

Sandra: Never. If it was me I'd tell.

Ashby: I was going to.

Phyllis: You lie.

Sandra: Too scared.

Ashby: I'm not.

Sandra: Go and tell her, then.

Ashby: I will.

Phyllis: Go on, then.

Ashby: I will.

Phyllis: He won't. Scared of the cane. She hits ever so hard.

Sandra: If you don't, I will.

(*She walks towards Meacher.*)

Ashby: I'm going.

(*He stands still.*)

Phyllis: Go on, then.

Sandra: He'll never do it.

Ashby: I will too. (*Still.*) Watch me.

(*He hesitates. They watch him.*)

I was going to anyway.

(*They watch him. He walks over to Meacher. Dexter moves away.*)

Morpeth (*Hardly audible*): Sir?

(*Dexter walks past. We hear Dexter's voice distantly.*)

Dexter: What's all this noise, Class 4?

(*Ashby coughts. Meacher is looking as the book.*)

Ashby: Miss?

Meacher: Mh. Yes, Eric?

Ashby: Miss, I . . . .

Meacher: What are you two girls hanging about for? You should be in your lessons.

(*Sandra and Phyllis exit.*)

Ashby: Miss.

Meacher: Yes?

Ashby: Miss, I . . . .

Meacher: Cough it up.

Ashby: Miss, you shouldn't cane Jacky Cropper, miss. It was me that pushed him. And it was me who wrote the letter, miss and everything, miss and . . .

Meacher: Stop.
   Eric Ashby. Didn't you have a fight with Jacky Cropper at the beginning of this term?

Ashby: Yes, Miss.

Meacher: And he won, didn't he?

Ashby: I suppose so, miss.

Meacher: Mh. I know what goes on in this school, Eric Ashby. I know who the bullies are. I know who the victims. Now, Cropper put you up to this, didn't he? Well?

Ashby: Miss, it was . . .

Meacher: Don't argue with me. He threatened you. He does that to a lot of the smaller boys. Now you mustn't be afraid of bullies, Eric. They're all cowards underneath. I'm glad you told me about this, because it will be the worse for him now.

Ashby: Miss, no . . . I . . .

Meacher: Off you go. And if he tries to do anything, you come and tell me about it, will you?
Off you go.

(*He goes. Stops. Turns. She points. He walks off. She watches him. Then she walks off.*)

Morpeth: Miss.

(*She doesn't hear him. She exits. Morpeth looks sad and desperate. The lights fade.*)

Dexter: Every week at this time we have 'I recommend'.

(*Lights up on Class 4.*)

You choose a book that you really enjoyed and tell us all about it. This week it's Sandra Linaker's turn. Sandra.

(*Sandra comes to the front.*)

Sandra: My book for 'I recommend' is called 'Angelique and the Pony Club Orphan' by Stella R. Fanshaw. I would award this book eight out of ten because it is all about horses. There are good characters and lots of adventure. I would recommend it to any boy or girl between ten and fourteen.
Shall I tell you about the story?

Dexter: Yes, go on Sandra.

Sandra: The main heroine is Angelique, who is thirteen with blue eyes and baby blonde hair. She is the captain of Sunnycliff Pony Club. Mr Dawlish wants to build a factory on the land where the Pony Club is. The only way they can stop him is by winning the Gymkhana.

(*The door opens and Ashby stands there. The class look at Ashby.*)

Angelique and Jim, the doctor's son, are chosen to compete in the Gymkhana but a week before, Jim breaks his leg and
. . . .

Dexter: Ashby!

Ashby: Been to see Miss Meacher, sir.

Dexter: I see. Sit down.

Sandra: Did you tell her?

Ashby: Course.

Sandra: Where's Cropper?

Ashby: I don't know.

Sandra: If you told her, he won't get caned.

Ashby: I said. I told her.

Dexter: Carry on, Sandra. Read a piece that you enjoyed.

Sandra: Sir, it's where Angelique's riding on the beach and it's four days before the Gymkhana and she runs over this boy, sir.

Dexter: Carry on.

Sandra: 'Angelique's blonde hair flew behind her in the wind. Her face clouded. Suddenly her horse reared and she saw the dark boy fall to the ground beneath the hooves. She leapt from her horse in one graceful, flowing motion. The boy stared up at her. His eyes were dark and seemed to be looking at a world that only he could see.
   "You won't give me up?" said the boy.
   There was something about the strange boy that frightened and at the same time fascinated her . . . .'

(*Cropper has entered. He looks round.*)

Dexter: It's a like a railway station in here. Where have you been?

Cropper: See Miss Meacher, sir.

(*Dexter goes to the table. Puts something in it.*)

Sergeant: What you get, Jacky, man? She cane you?

Cropper: Six.

Trask: Six!

Cropper: Each hand.

Sergeant: Six. Did she hurt you?

Cropper: She couldn't hurt me.

Irene: Didn't Ashby say it was him?

Cropper: Ashby?

Sandra: Said he'd tell Meacher it was him.

Cropper: Ashby? He never said nothing.

Dexter: Sit down now, Cropper. Where were we? Who can tell me?

Irene: Sir, sir. This girl Angela who has blonde hair and baby blue eyes is galloping across the beach and she knocks over this boy because she's not looking where she's going 'cos she's thinking about the race thing they're going in for . . .

Dexter: At least someone is listening. Carry on, Sandra.

Cropper: Six on each hand, Ashby. I'm going to get you.

Dexter: Sandra.

Trask: You're bleeding, Croppy. You could tell the cops on her.

Sandra: ' "Give you up?" said Angelique. "Why should I? Come on, I'll take you home." '

(*Lights fade but a spot remains on Sandra. All but Ashby and Sandra sit quietly.*)

'The boy turned his head from her. There was bitterness in his mouth and his gypsy eyes were dark, wounded and yet full of bitter pride.
    'They turned full on Angelique.'

Ashby: Home. What home?

Sandra: ' . . . he said. There was a sadness in him deeper than Angelique had ever seen in any person's eyes. Angelique spoke softly. "To your mother," she said, "I'll take you home to your mother." '

(*Spot up on Ashby.*)

Ashby: My mother? You won't find my mother at home . . .

Sandra: ' . . . said the boy. "Where is she?" asked Angelique.'

Ashby: She died. She was in an accident a year ago. That's why I'm in the orphanage. I ran away. They beat me once too often. I'd die rather than go back there.

Sandra: ' "Look," cried Angelique, "why don't you come back with me? I can hide you in the barn. They'll never find you there." She leapt on to her horse's back and extended her hand. "Come on."
    'The strange boy leapt up agilely behind her and they galloped across the beach. The horse's hooves pattered in the shallow waters and the sky behind was dark. Dark as the eyes of the gypsy youth.'

(*The lights fade up. The class has gone. Sandra is there upstage and to the right of Ashby.*)

Ashby: It's the truth.

Sandra: You mean — she's really dead.

Ashby: Wouldn't tell lies about that, would I?

Sandra: Even if Meacher asked you?

Ashby: Course not. It's all true. Honest.

Sandra: I've never known anyone whose mum died before.

(*Pause.*)

Ashby: I don't know if you've noticed, but I sometimes have this faraway look. In the eyes. It's because of that.

Sandra: Have you told anybody else?

Ashby: No.

Sandra: I'm the first one?

Ashby: Yeah.

Sandra: If you're lying . . . if it's not true . . . .

Ashby: It is. It is, honest.

Sandra: But if it's not, you know what'll happen. Your mum'll die. It'll be your fault. It's like what Dexter told us. It will be like you killed her. Killed your own mum.

(*Sergeant runs up with Irene behind him.*)

Sergeant: What you doing here?

Sandra: Go away, you — Eric's telling me about . . .

Ashby: Don't tell him. Don't tell anybody.

Irene: What? What hasn't he to tell?

Sandra: You mind your own business.

Sergeant: Jacky Cropper's looking for you, Ashby. He's going to bash you. Are you scared, man? Have I to tell him where you are?

Ashby: Yeah. Tell him where I am.

Sergeant: Come on.

(*Sergeant and Irene dash off.*)

Sandra: Are you going to fight him?

Ashby: I suppose so.

Sandra: D'you want my photo? You can have it if you like.

Ashby: Can I?

Sandra: I've got plenty. I don't think it's very good.

(*Sergeant runs on, speaking as he comes.*)

Sergeant: He's coming. Cropper's coming.

(*Cropper enters. The rest trailing behind curiously.*)

Cropper: You been hiding?

Ashby: I'm not hiding.

Cropper: Course you were.

Ashby: Why should I hide from you?

Cropper: 'Cos I'm going to murder you. Think you're clever don't you?

Ashby: Doesn't take much to be cleverer than you.

Cropper: What you say?

Ashby: A donkey could do that.

Cropper: I'll get you.

(*Thumps him to the floor.*)

Get up, you.

Sandra: You can't fight him. His mum . . .

Cropper: His mum. We all know about her.

Ashby: Shut up, you!

Cropper: She's been seen. We saw her with someone and it wasn't your dad.

Ashby: Shut up, Cropper.

Cropper: My dad says she's no better than she ought to be.

Ashby: You shut up about my mum.

(*He hurls himself on Cropper. They roll on the floor. The others crowd round.*)

All: Fight! Fight!

(*A whistle blows and Dexter enters.*)

Dexter: Get up. Get up, both of you.
(*He drags them to their feet. They glower.*)
Now. What's all this about?

Ashby: It was him, sir, he said about my mum . . .

Cropper: It was only true.

Ashby: You!

(*Goes for him again.*)

Dexter: Stop it! You know my rules. I warned you. After school. Get the gloves on. Settle it like men. 4.15 sharp. Understood?

Cropper:
Ashby: } Yes sir.

Dexter: All right, clear off, the rest of you. Come along.

(*Dexter exits. Cropper sidles off with backward glances.*)

Cropper: You wait.

Ashby: Yeah.

Cropper: You wait and see, that's all.

Ashby: You an' all.

Cropper: You just wait, that's all. I'll get you.

(*Meacher enters.*)

Ashby: Like to see.

Cropper: You'll see.

(*Ashby and Sandra look at each other.*)

Meacher: Ah, there you are, Eric Ashby. I've got a message for you. It's from the hospital. It's about your mother.

(*Sandra and Ashby look at each other. Lights fade.*)

The children (*In turn*):

You heard.
Who?
Ashby. Eric Ashby.
His mum.
What happened?
Ashby's mum?
Sandra Linaker said.
She was there.

His mum died.
How did she die?
Ashby.
He killed her.
He's in Meacher's room.
They sent for the police.
They took him away.
Ashby done it?
He killed her.
Sandra said. He told her.
Ashby's a murderer.
He told me.
And me.
And me.
And me.

(*The voices fade. Knocking at a door.*
   Lights up on Miss Meacher's office. Meacher sits at her desk.
There is a chair in front of it. A knock.)

Meacher: Come in.

(*Ashby enters and stands by the door.*)

Eric Ashby. I wanted to see you.
Come over here.

(*He crosses.*)

Well. You've been getting yourself into some scrapes.
   I remember you in the first year. Your mother bringing you
in. You liked it here then. That first day, your mother said
you even wanted to come back to school after tea. Do you
remember?

Ashby: No, miss.

Meacher: Mh. What's happened?

Ashby: Dunno, miss.

Meacher: What's all this about?

Ashby: All what, miss?

Meacher: Don't pretend to be stupid with me, Eric Ashby.
You know what I'm talking about.
This fighting you've got yourself into.

Ashby: It was Jacky Cropper.

Meacher: It can't be just Cropper. Otherwise he'd be hitting
himself. Takes two to make a fight.

Ashby: He said something, miss.

Meacher: What did he say?

Ashby: Can't remember, miss.

Meacher: I can't help you if you don't tell me. And I am here
to help you. (*Pause.*) Now what did he say?

Ashby: Something about . . .

Meacher: About whom?

Ashby: Miss, about me mum, miss.

Meacher: What did he say about your mum?

Ashby: Things, miss.

Meacher: He said something not very nice about your mum.

Ashby: Miss.

Meacher: So you hit him.

Ashby: Yes, miss.

Meacher: He's bigger than you.

Ashby: Yes, miss.

Meacher: Older than you. Stronger than you. And he knows how to fight.

Ashby: Yes, miss.

Meacher: Why don't you pick on someone your own size?

Ashby: Miss?

Meacher: Mr Dexter stopped it. Who was winning?

Ashby: I had him on the floor, miss and I was . . .

Meacher: Who was winning?

(*Pause.*)

Ashby: He was, miss.

Meacher: Well. Sit down, Eric.

(*He sits.*)

Your father rang. It's about your mother. He said she'd been taken to hospital.

Ashby: Hospital, miss.

Meacher: He said.

(*Ashby is bent over. He sobs.*)

Eric?

Ashby: I didn't mean it, miss. I didn't mean her to . . . didn't mean to kill her . . . I just said it . . . I just said it because of Sandra. I didn't mean to kill her . . .

Meacher: What are you talking about?

(*Ashby continues to cry.*)

Have you got a hankie?

(*He shakes his head.*)

Here.

(*She gives him one. He wipes his face. Blows his nose.*)

Now. She's been taken to hospital. It's just that your father won't be in when you get home. He says you're to go to Mrs Jarman's at thirty-one for your tea. Do you know Mrs Jarman?

Ashby: Lives at thirty-one, miss.

Meacher: That's all.

Ashby: Miss, she's not going to die then?

Meacher: Die? Well, if she does she'll be the first person I know to die of a broken ankle.

Ashby: Ankle ... But ...

(*He stares.*)

Meacher: You can keep the hankie. I'm sorry I haven't got one without frills.

Ashby: Will she be all right, miss?

Meacher: Of course. She'll probably be better for the rest. She hasn't been at home for some time, has she?

Ashby: No, miss.

Meacher: Do you know why? Has your dad spoken about it with you?

Ashby: She's been away. On holiday, miss. (*An obvious lie.*)

Meacher: On holiday?

Ashby: Yes, miss.

Meacher: I see. (*Pause.*) Well, now she's back from holiday. Once she gets out of hospital you'll be pleased to see her back, I should think.

Ashby: Yes, miss.

Meacher: So that's all right, isn't it?
Now you have been in some scrapes. What's all this about Sandra?

Ashby: Just something I said, miss.

Meacher: And this letter you wrote.

Ashby: Me, miss.

Meacher: Of course. It was you, wasn't it?

Ashby: Yes, miss. But Cropper . . .

Meacher: He couldn't have written that. He can't spell that well.

Ashby: But you caned him, miss.

Meacher: No I didn't. I might have felt like it, but . . .

Ashby: He said you gave him six.

Meacher: Did he?

Ashby: On each hand. He told everybody.

Meacher: Well, you can tell them that I didn't. And if they don't believe you, you can send them to me.
Now about this letter and the ten-shilling note . . . .

Ashby: And it was me pushed him in the photo, miss.

Meacher: Did you? Why?

Ashby: He said something, miss . . . .

Meacher: About . . . Oh I can't go through all that again. Eric, you must try to stop hitting people every time they say something you don't like.

Now, about this letter. Handwriting's improved. At least we've taught you something while you've been here. (*She reads over the letter silently.*) You know, if I was Sandra I wouldn't have . . . . . .

Well, there it is.

(*For a moment she is no longer the intimidating Headmistress. She turns towards the window. Looks out for a second. Silence. Eric is looking at her. She turns back to him.*)

There it is . . . . You better have the letter back. It is yours, isn't it? Unless you want to give it to Sandra. Well you can sort that out with her. It's your business really, isn't it? I shall speak to Mr Dexter. About this fight. Are you frightened?

Ashby: No . . . yes, miss. No.

Meacher: Mh. Not very pleasant to be punched by someone like Cropper. It might hurt a good deal, I shouldn't wonder. You know I can't really have people going about hurting each other in my school. Why don't you ask him to shake hands? Let byegones be byegones. Bury the hatchet.

Ashby: Couldn't, miss.

Meacher: That's what I thought you'd say. You'd rather get a thrashing. His father's a boxer, you know.

Ashby: I know, miss.

Meacher: Doesn't seem fair, does it? I think I ought to stop it.

Ashby: Stop it, miss?

Meacher: I can you know. I only have to say.

Ashby: Miss, Mr Dexter . . .

Meacher: Don't you worry about Mr Dexter. You leave Mr Dexter to me. (*Pause.*) Well? You want me to have it stopped?

Ashby: No, miss.

Meacher: You're making it difficult for me to help you, Eric Ashby. Ever had boxing lessons?

Ashby: Miss?

Meacher: Put up your hand.

Ashby: Miss?

Meacher: Go on. Put it up. Open the palm.

(*Ashby does so. Meacher unleashes a right hook that explodes into Ashby's open palm.*)

Meacher: That's called a right hook.
My father taught me that. I was bullied at school. I was, well . . . wore glasses. Bit of a sight really . . . sometimes others pick on you . . . Look, let's see you try.

(*Ashby tries.*)

Again. Bend the knees. That's where the strength is. Let the shoulder come through. As though the whole side of your body was punching. Again.

(*Ashby tries again.*)

Well. You can't learn it in five minutes. You want to go on with this?

Ashby: Yes, miss.

Meacher: Mh. Well, you'll just have to do the best you can. Try to keep out of reach. Are you sure you don't want me to stop ... No all right, off you go. There's no need to tell anyone about what's been said. Or the ... er ... hook. Don't use it on anybody else. I don't want anyone getting hurt.

(*Ashby exits. Meacher stares out. He has left the letter. She sees it. Picks it up. Reads it. Looks up and faraway.
Dexter's voice across her reverie. She does not react to it.*)

Dexter: If you want to be part of this just behave properly.

(*A bell rings harshly. The lights fades on Meacher. Comes up on a square formed by children.*)

All right. Simmer down. If you're staying, sit down. This is a three-round contest, each round being of three minutes' duration. There will be a half-minute rest between rounds. I am the referee. My decision is final. Now, in the blue corner on my left, Jacky Cropper.

(*Cropper in singlet and shorts rises and prances throwing punches. Applause from his supporters.*)

And in the red corner —

(*The red corner is empty.*)

Ashby? Where's Ashby?

Cropper: Too scared to turn up, sir.

(*Catcalls and cheers.*)

Dexter: That'll do. We'll give him five minutes. If he's not here by then he'll have forfeited the contest.

Trask: Saw him running down the road, sir. (*Laughter from the 'crowd'.*) Crying his eyes out.

Sergeant: Ten, nine, eight, seven . . .

Dexter: Stop that! You'll behave like gentlemen or you can go home.

Cropper: Sir, he's not coming, sir.

Sergeant: Here he is, sir.

(*Ashby enters. He's wearing shorts and a vest and black plimsolls. He wears his jacket over his shoulders.*)

Dexter: Ah, there you are, Ashby. We've been waiting for you.

Trask: To be knocked out.

(*Laughter. Dexter brings Cropper and Ashby together.*)

Dexter: Now remember to protect yourself at all times. And to come out fighting. May the best man win.

Trask: Yeah, Cropper, with a knockout.

Dexter: Now shake hands.

Trask: That's the last time Ashby'll touch him.

(*They retire to their corners. Cropper jigs about. Ashby stands waiting.*)

Dexter: Seconds out.

Cropper: Haven't got any seconds, sir.

Dexter: Timekeeper.

(*Morpeth rings a bell. Shouts of encouragement from the crowd.*)

Ashby's Adult Voice (*Voice over as they fight*):   I tried to remember all the things I'd been told about boxing. I stuck my left fist straight out and covered my face with the other.

(*The fight could be in slow motion. In a red light, or a strobe.*)

Cropper was good. He danced around on his toes. Throwing out lefts.

Trask: Go on, kill him, Cropper.

(*Ashby falls from a blow.*)

Ashby's Adult Voice: His fist got through and hit me on the side of the head. It made my ear ring. I was deaf on one side for a week.

(*Ashby gets up.*)

I tried to hit him but he just ducked and dodged out of the way. When he came for me the next time I ducked as well. But I dodged straight into his left fist.

(*Ashby falls then gets up.*)

My nose was bleeding. I put both gloves over my face.

(*Ashby is hit in the belly. He falls.*)

He hit me right in the stomach. I couldn't breathe. The next thing I was on the floor.

(*He falls again.*)

I didn't see what hit me. I couldn't see at all. Then I saw him dancing around in front of me. I felt like you do when you're going to fall down in a faint, except I was on the floor already. Cropper really knew how to punch.

I wasn't going to stay down. I pulled myself up. I didn't seem to have any strength in my arms.

(*He gets up.*)

But then I was up. I still couldn't see properly. I could see him. See him dancing and feinting but it was like I was looking through one of those glazed windows.

(*A blow to the head from Cropper.*)

He thumped me again across the head.

Dexter: Had enough, Ashby? (*Dexter's voice could be distorted on the tape.*)

(*Ashby falls again.*)

Ashby: I fell down again. If he hit me once more, it would be the end.

(*Ashby gets up.*)

I couldn't even raise the strength to put my gloves up. I saw Cropper drawing back his fist. 'Hit me, Cropper', I thought. 'Let's get it over with.' I closed my eyes . . .

Meacher (*Calling from the back of the room*):   That's enough! Stop the fight. I won't have this kind of brutality in my school.

Dexter: But, Miss Meacher.

Meacher: No buts, Mr Dexter. Send everybody home.

Ashby's Adult Voice: Then I thought I heard her tell me something. Maybe imagined it. I swear she was talking to me.

(*Meacher's voice in a whisper on tape.*)

Meacher: The hook, Eric. The left hook.

Ashby's Adult Voice: I gathered up all my strength.

Dexter: You heard what Miss Meacher said. Everybody home.

Cropper: Oh sir, that's not fair.

(*Cropper drops his guard and turns away.*)

I was just going to knock him out. I . . .

(*He turns back to Ashby as if to continue the fight and walks into a right hook that Ashby brings up from the floor. Cropper collapses to the floor, unconscious. As Ashby steps back from the body of Cropper the action could change back to slow motion. Dexter raises Cropper. The children rise and pick up their coats and put them on. They begin to make their way out towards the sides and rear, crossing one another.*)

Meacher (*On tape.***):**   Perhaps I did say it. Perhaps I just wanted to and you heard it. It wouldn't do, would it, for a Headmistress to encourage her children to knock each other out.

(*Sandra is waiting for Ashby. He stops then walks past her. Meacher's voice is continuous with the action. The children hum the opening song softly. She comes to the front after looking after Eric for a while. At the end he is left upstage right, still, and she is standing down centre.*)

Don't come and see me. I don't want you to see me now. I wonder what happened to you all. I kept your letter you know. In a way I suppose I was jealous of her. That's funny, isn't it? Being jealous of an eleven-year-old girl. I suppose she has children of her own now. I often think back. Think about you all. It isn't easy being what I was either. I wish sometimes I could be eleven again. I often think of that. Eleven again and a bit prettier than I was. Not too much, just enough and perhaps someday a boy would ask me if he could walk me home from school. Past the barber's shop, the Co-op, the Institute. It would be nice to be eleven and have an ordinary, dull day in front of you. Nothing exciting, just an ordinary dull day. It wouldn't even matter if it was raining, you know. So, just think about me sometimes now and again. Not if you're busy. Sometime when you have nothing better to do. I'd like to think of you doing that. If you could manage it for me now and then, I'd really like that a lot.

(*She looks out, not unhappily, yet not smiling. All the children are 'frozen'. Eric is isolated and Irene is close but not too close. The lights have faded until just a spot is on Miss Meacher. It stays on her dimly for three seconds at the conclusion of her last word and then fades to blackout and the play ends.*

If there is to be a curtain the cast should assemble for the photograph as in the opening scene. Still.)

Activities

Don't look down is written as a stage play, but it could also be presented as a film. Before you put on a performance of the play, first work through these exercises.

Thinking about the characters

1 Produce a character card for each of the main characters. On one side write a pen portrait of him/her giving a description of his/her character as it is revealed by what he/she does in the play. On the other side, write a profile of him/her — similar to the profiles you see in magazines — in which you use your imagination and give details of such things as the character's likes and dislikes, hopes and fears. You could, if you want, include drawings on the cards.

2 In pairs, role-play an interview with one of the main characters. Before you begin, make a list of questions to ask about why the character behaved as he/she did and what he/she was thinking at key points in the play. For example, here are two questions you could ask Ashby: Why did you tell Sandra that your mum was dead? How did you feel when you went to tell Miss Meacher that it was you who wrote the letter?

3 a) Choose one of the main characters. Pick out a scene in which the character is involved. Take a piece of paper and divide it into two columns. In one column list what the character says and does in that scene. In the other column say what you learn about the character from his/her behaviour in the scene.

b) Join up with a partner and discuss what each of you has written. Then, choose another scene in which the character is involved and repeat the exercise.

4 Which are the most important scenes in the play? Choose one of them. Work in a group and either read it or act it out. Before you begin, select two key points in the scene when you are going to 'freeze' the action. At these points get each member of the group to take it in turns to speak in role and to say what their character is thinking at that particular moment.

5 What comments do you think Mr Dexter and/or Miss Meacher would have written on the children's reports? Choose two of the children. Write the comments that Mr Dexter and Miss Meacher would write on their reports. Then, form groups and discuss what you have written.

6 Work with a partner. Improvise and then write the script of an extra scene involving two of the characters. For example, you could write the script of a scene between Miss Meacher and Jacky Cropper.

7 The play is presented as if Ashby is thinking back to his schooldays. What memories of the incidents he recalls do you think Jacky Cropper or Sandra Linaker would have as adults? As if you are Jacky or Sandra, write a monologue (a long speech made by one actor in a play, especially when alone) beginning: 'Yes, I remember her — Miss Meacher — and that Eric Ashby . . .'

Thinking about the situations

1 The director of a production of the play has asked you to write the programme notes, saying what the play is about. Write 200 words about what happens in the play. Before you begin, work in pairs or groups and discuss what the play is about.

2 a) 'Although the play is set in an English school in 1948, it deals with the types of situation that many children experience.' Do you agree with this statement? Does the play deal with 'typical situations'? Talk about the situations that occur in the play. As you read it, did it remind you of any situations that you yourself had experienced?

b) In groups, develop a role-play based on a situation similar to one of the situations in the play.

Presenting the play

1 The action of the play takes place in 1948. In order to be able to design the set, to make the costumes and to collect the properties you need, first of all you will have to find out what schools such as Mary Street School were like. Using the resources in your school and local library, find out all you can about schools in England in the years immediately after the end of the Second World War. Study pictures of the classrooms and of the children and teachers. Makes notes on the general appearance of the classrooms, the desks, the children's satchels and pens, the children's clothes and the teachers' clothes. Then, a) draw a set plan to fit your stage or drama studio, b) design costumes for the pupils and teachers and c) read the play through carefully and make a list of all the properties you will need.

2 In his introductory note, the author of the play, Gareth Owen says: 'The action of the play should appear to be continuous, rather like that of a film.' How are you going to achieve this? By dividing up your acting area and leaving part of it set up as a classroom throughout the whole play? By presenting some of the action on the apron (the part of the stage in front of the curtain), while a scene-change goes on behind the curtain? By training a team of scene-shifters to move furniture, such as desks, on and off the stage quickly and unobtrusively between scenes? By a combination of these and/ or other methods? In pairs, study the play and make a list of the various scenes and scene-changes. Discuss each scene-change in turn and suggest ways of making the action as continuous as possible, bearing in mind the restrictions of the space and equipment available to you in your hall or drama studio.

3 Gareth Owen stresses that it is vital that the events should
be portrayed seriously and that any humour should arise out of
the realism. It is important too that each of the children should
be presented as an individual and not as a caricature or
stereotype. Before you cast the play, work in a group and
produce casting notes on each of the characters. Your casting
notes should state clearly what you think the person is like and
what impression anyone playing the part should try to give of
that character. Discuss what you think the physical appearance
of each character should be and what sort of voice she/he
should have.

4   Before you begin rehearsals, look at each scene in turn and
identify any particular problems that you might have in staging
it. For example, how are you going to stage the fight between
Ashby and Cropper? Discuss possible ways of dramatising key
moments in the fight.

Writing your own scripts

1 In the first and final scenes of *Don't look down*, Gareth
Owen uses the technique of making one of the main
characters, Ashby, speak as an adult, so that the events of the
play are presented as if they were a sequence of memories.
Write a script of your own, set in a school, in which the events
are introduced by one of the characters speaking as an adult.

2 Gareth Owen begins the play with the cast on stage posing
for the school photograph. He uses this device as a way of
setting the scene and of introducing the characters, firstly by
getting some of them — Miss Meacher and Sandra — to
introduce themselves by speaking directly to the audience and
secondly by bringing the scene to life. Write the script of a

scene which begins with the characters on stage posing for a photograph. It could be any kind of photograph — an official photograph, a holiday snap, a photo taken on a school trip or a photograph posed for a newspaper.

3 Gareth Owen uses the classroom scenes to enable him to show the children's thoughts and feelings not only through what they say to each other and the teacher, but also by what they write and what they read. In Mr Dexter's composition lesson, the children read out what they write on the theme of 'What I want to be when I grow up'. Discuss how he uses the 'I recommend' lesson in a similar way. Then, write a short play of your own, set in a school. Include a classroom scene and use what happens in the lesson to get your characters to tell the audience more about themselves, e.g. by reading aloud their compositions on a topic such as 'What I'm afraid of' or 'A time when I was very angry', or by each giving a short talk to the class on a topic of their own choice.

4: Unsung

DAVID FOXTON

The characters

BARRY WAKEFIELD
CHARLIE TAYLOR
PRIMARY TEACHER
'SPECKY' WILKINSON (later a BUS CONDUCTOR)
'ROBBO' ROBINSON
SAMANTHA MORTON
'FATTY' WOTHERSPOON
TOM
TIM
LARRY
HARRY
TEACHER 1
TEACHER 2
BARRY'S MOTHER
BARRY'S DAD
ANDY
BRI
CHRIS
ANN HARDY
SUSAN ARKWRIGHT
NEIGHBOUR 1
NEIGHBOUR 2
HEADMASTER
MR SUMMERS
MR COSTELLO
SERGEANT
CAPTAIN
BBC NEWSCASTER

The cast should act as a backing to all the scenes of the play. This can be achieved by their sitting in a semi-circle with the scenes being played within the semi-circle, and the chairs can be used to create the suggestion of the various locations; e.g. a cinema, an office, the interior of a bus, etc. In some scenes non-speaking members of the cast become a crowd, an audience, fellow-travellers, etc. All properties should be mimed.

(As the curtain opens the cast sing to the tune 'Billy, Don't be a Hero':

> Barry don't be a hero, don't be a fool all your life
> Barry don't be a hero, make it a rule of your life.
> And as Barry started to grow
> They said 'Keep your ambitions low'
> Barry don't be a hero, be just like me.

Barry breaks forward and speaks to the audience.)

Barry: The youngest established age at which someone was awarded the Victoria Cross — a decoration awarded for conspicuous bravery to members of British and British Commonwealth armed forces, first instituted by Queen Victoria in 1856 and struck from metal of guns captured at Sebastopol during the Crimean War — is 15 years and 3 months — Apprentice Arthur Fitzgibbon.
    That's what I wanted to be.

Charlie: What — an apprentice?

Barry: Charlie never bothered to listen. Even in primary school he never listened.

(Scene: the Primary School: the cast sing a snatch of 'Lavender Blue'.)

Charlie: Give us some of your Plasticine, Barry!

Barry: Miss said we had to use what we were given and no more, she said.

Charlie: I can't finish my man-eating monster if I don't get some — come on, lend us some.

Barry: Miss said . . .

Charlie: Aw! Come on . . . what you making, anyway?

Barry: Victoria Cross.

Charlie: Never heard of her, who is she?

Barry: It's a medal — a cross pattee of bronze with the Royal Crown surmounted by a lion in the centre and, beneath, the inscription 'For Valour'.

Primary Teacher: Now then, Barry Wakefield, let's see what you've been doing. Oh, my goodness, is that all you've managed this morning? Charles has made a lovely man-eating monster, and Sarah-Jane's made a little Wendy house, with doors that open, and even Jeremy's made a whole family of snakes . . . and here you are with nothing to show for the entire morning except a rolled-out piece of Plasticine with squiggles all over it. I think I know someone who can't be trusted to arrange the conkers on our nature table.

Barry: And she didn't let me play in the sand-tray.

Primary teacher: And you certainly won't play in the sand-tray.

Barry: Pity, that! I was going to do El' Alamein, and be Monty himself. Charlie would be Rommel — if he'd listen to instructions.

Primary Teacher: I really don't know what you're going to be when you grow up.

Barry: I always knew what I wanted to be when I grew up. There was never never any doubt about it. Charlie wanted to be a Frankenstein's monster . . . (*Charlie mimes and freezes.*) . . . but *I* didn't.

My friend Specky Wilkinson wanted to be an engine driver . . . (*'Specky' shunts on as a train and freezes.*) . . . but *I* didn't!

'Robbo' Robinson said he wanted to be a professional footballer . . . (*'Robbo' dribbles on, passes, and freezes.*) . . . but *I* didn't!

Samantha Morton said she wanted to be a fashion model — but you don't get boys doing things like that! (*Samantha's entrance is stopped by Barry.*)

'Fatty' Wotherspoon wanted to be a private detective . . . (*'Fatty' sleuths on and freezes.*) . . . but *I* didn't!

Tom (*Entering and miming and freezing*): . . . A clown?

Barry: No!

Tim (*Entering and miming and freezing*): . . . A policeman?

Barry: No!

Larry (*Entering and miming and freezing*): . . . A pop star?

Barry: No!

Harry (*Entering and miming and freezing*): . . . A vicar?

Barry: No!
(*To audience*) Nobody could ever guess. It was a secret! I didn't tell anyone. Nobody knew. Except *me*!

(The freeze breaks and the others gather round Barry asking 'What you gonna be, Barry?', 'Tell us, Barry?', 'What's the secret, Barry?', 'Come on'. Then they make guesses — 'a deep sea diver', 'a brain surgeon', 'an airline pilot', 'a king', 'an artist's model', 'a hairdresser', 'a bus conductress' (they could become even sillier). They taunt him and eventually he gives in, and tells them.)

Barry: All right, I'll tell you — a hero!

(Pause. Then they laugh and ad-lib scornful comments.)

Barry *(Erupting)*: Stop it! Stop it! All of you. It's not fair, why shouldn't I be a hero?

(They all freeze except Barry.)

Barry *(To audience)*: Why not? Eh? Why not? Someone has to do it! And there weren't any heroes up our street. Not one! My dad always said that Harry Evans was a hero having to put up with Mrs Evans — but I don't think he meant it really! It was just because Mrs Evans was a big fat lady! And old Mr Bolton had been in the war — at least he said that was why he limped — but my mum said he'd been run over by a tram in the blackout, and my dad said the only medal he'd been given was the Naafi medal for standing in the tea queue — so perhaps it wasn't shrapnel at all!

But I wished I'd never told anyone. Everybody seemed to find out!

(Scene: the High School — Staffroom.)

Teacher 1: Seen anything of the new first year yet?

Teacher 2: Enough.

Teacher 1: What do they teach them in primary school these days?

Teacher 2: Less and less!

Teacher 1: And we have to pick up the pieces. Have you met this kid ... Wakefield ... Bernard ... or Barry Wakefield?

Teacher: 2: No — why?

Teacher 1: Needs an educational psychologist — a definite case for the shrink ... claims he wants to be a hero.

Teacher 2: Hero, eh? Well, he's come to the right place.

Barry: It's hard to become a hero when everyone knows you want to be one. No one takes you seriously.

(*Scene: the Playing Field.*)

Teacher 2: Come on, Wakefield, tackle me, tackle me!

(*Barry fails abysmally.*)

Teacher 2: Not quite a Roy of the Rovers, are you, Wakefield? Not quite a hero of the centre circle, eh?

Barry: I think I've twisted my ankle.

Teacher 2: Spoken like a man of superhuman strength, courage, or ability, favoured by the gods! Move yourself, Wakefield.

Barry: And it's even harder to become a hero when your *mum* knows you want to be one.

(*Scene: Barry's Home.*)

Mother: Come on, our Barry! It's time you were up! Heroes don't lie in bed on Saturday mornings.

Barry: When do they lie in bed?

Mother: Don't be cheeky! It's time you were up! I won't tell you again.

Barry: But she did!

Mother: Eat your crusts, Barry.

Barry: But I don't like them, Mum.

Mother: You'll never be a hero if you don't eat your crusts up. How can you hope to grow up big and strong?

Barry: Heroes don't have to be big and strong.

Mother: Of course they do — who told you otherwise?

Barry: I read it in a book.

Mother: Well, I bet Winston Churchill always ate his crusts up. And Horatio Nelson. And I'll bet Scott of the Antarctic's mother didn't have to stand over him at breakfast times, to get him to eat his Frosties . . .

(*Barry gets up to go.*)

And where are you going now?

Barry: I'm just going out — I may be some time! (*To audience*) My mother didn't understand.

(*Scene: outside Barry's House.*)

Charlie: Are you ready then, Barry?

Barry: Ready?

Charlie: *Flash Gordon* . . . come on, I'll see you inside.

Barry (*To audience*): Saturday-morning pictures at the Bug-Hutch.

Mother: Barry! Barry! Have you finished your breakfast?

Barry: Yes thanks, Mum!

Mother (*To audience*):   He's not eating enough breakfast . . .
you can't be a hero on an empty stomach, can you? I don't
know — I wish I understood that boy . . . I don't know who
he takes after . . . but it's no one in my family I can tell you
that!

(*Dad 'sword-fences' on.*)

Barry: Morning, Errol Flynn!

Dad: And where do you think you're sloping off to, our Barry?

Barry: Going to the Bug-Hutch, Dad! Pictures! It's Saturday-
morning pictures!

Dad: Aren't you getting a bit old for that these days?

(*He 'fences' more.*)

Barry: How d'you mean, D'Artagnan?

Dad: It's for kids! Little kids! You're growing up, Barry!

Barry: But it's *Flash Gordon*, Dad.

Dad: It's rubbish, more like! You'd be a lot better off helping
me down the allotment.

Barry: It's the last episode, Dad — *The Curse of Ming!*

Dad: It's a curse all right! You'll never be a hero if you go to
the pictures on Saturday mornings.

(*He 'fences' more.*)

Barry: I don't think that my Dad, the Douglas Fairbanks of
Hope Street, understood either.

Dad: You'd learn more by helping me, our Barry!

Barry: Barry Wakefield — the rhubarb hero — champion of the Westmoor allotments.

Dad: Are you coming then, Superman?

Barry: Next week! Next week!

Dad: I don't give pocket money to heroes who won't dig the garden, and we've got that tree to chop down some time!

Barry: George Washington never had this problem.

(*He moves off towards the cinema.*)

(*Scene: the Street.*)

Andy: Where are you off to, Barry Wakefield?

Barry: Pictures!

Bri: What for?

Barry: A haircut, what d'you think?

Bri: Watch it, you, or I'll give you a thumpin'.

Barry: You and whose army?

Bri: I'm warnin' you!

Andy: Leave off him!

Bri: You shut up an' all! I reckon it's time someone gave him a real bashin'.

Chris: Leave him alone.

Barry: Come on then! Come on! I've got five minutes before the pictures start. What are you waitin' for?

Bri: Right! You've asked for it!

Chris: Now's your chance to be a hero, Barry.

Bri: Come on — ready when you are!

Chris: And in the Blue Corner at five stone, wet through, that well-known would-be hero Barry 'Bone-cruncher' Wakefield.

Bri: Stop all that! Just let me get at him.

Chris: Versus 'Killer' Goodwin from Gaitskill Avenue.

Barry: I'm not scared of him!

Chris: Course you're not — you're a hero after all!

Barry: Not yet I'm not!

Andy: You will be after all this lot.

Chris: What d' you mean?

Andy: Facing up to Goodwin — he'll be a right hero at school.

Barry: I've got to make a start somewhere!

Bri: Just a minute — what was that you said?

Barry: Me?

Bri: No, him. (*Indicates Andy.*) What did you say about being a hero?

Andy: I said that Barry'll be a hero at school — after fighting you.

Bri: Oh, will he?

Chris: I should think so!

Bri: Right then — I'm not fightin' — I'm not interested any
  more! Get yourself another mug!

Barry: Come on! Put 'em up! What are you so scared of?

Bri: You're not making a fool out of me! No way!

  (*Bri, Chris and Andy drift off.*)

Barry: Come back! Come on! I'm ready for you! I'm not
  scared! I'm not bothered about you, Goodwin. You don't
  scare me! I'll cripple you! I'll mullycrush you! I'll pulverise
  you! I'll spifflercate you! 'Killer'? Rubbish! Come on then!
  I'll knock the living daylights out of you! I am the
  champion! I am the greatest! The best! Amazing! Supreme!

Ann: I always thought heroes were modest, Barry Wakefield?

  (*Pause.*)

  Come on, we'll be late for *Flash Gordon*.

Barry (*To audience***):** I didn't always go to the pictures with
  Ann.

Ann (*To audience***):** He did on Saturday mornings.

Barry: Well, she brought the mint imperials!

Ann: . . . and the fruit gums.

Barry: Yes . . .

Ann: . . . and the crisps . . .

Barry: Yes . . .

Ann: . . . cheese and onion . . .

Barry: Not always!

Ann: Well, sometimes they were salt and vinegar.

Barry: That's why I went with her.

Ann: . . . and because you were scared of the dark!

Barry: It isn't true. Ooh! You do tell lies, Ann Hardy! . . . and anyway I didn't pay for her . . .

Ann: I always thought that heroes were generous, Barry Wakefield.

Barry: Only those that dig the garden, my Dad says!

Ann: Come on! We don't want to be late . . . I said I'd meet Susan inside.

Barry: Oh no! Not Susan Arkwright! Why didn't you tell me before?

Ann: I forgot.

Barry: Arkwright the 'Orrible. A mouth on legs! She'll never stop talking! And she'll tell everybody I was out with Ann. Oh heck. Just my luck to meet the Mouth of the Month.

Ann: Come on, Barry! What're you waiting for?

Barry (*Stoically*): It is a far, far better thing I do than I have ever done before. It is a far, far better rest I go to . . .

Ann (*Dragging him off*): . . . Come on — Danger Mouse!

(*Scene: in the Cinema.*)

Susan: I tell you! It were that funny . . . I'd said I'd go to the Saturday pictures with Ann Hardy — you know — her whose father runs that betting-shop on the corner of Price Street. Well I went . . . and she said to meet her inside . . . so I were there with me bag of midget gems and some kayli . . . and I waited and waited . . . and I thought she weren't going to turn up . . . and there were these lads behind and they kept making comments . . . and pulling me plaits . . . and I told them to stop . . . and one of them was that big spotty kid from Mrs Henshaw's class . . . but he just laughed . . . and I was just about to go and . . . when Ann comes in (*She does*) . . . with Barry Wakefield with her . . . I was that surprised . . . and he sat with us . . . all the way through . . . and when *Flash Gordon* was on he kept shutting me up . . . all the time . . . he wouldn't let me talk. I finished all me midget gems and most of me kayli 'cos he kept saying 'Ssh!' . . . and I think he held hands with Ann as well . . . I couldn't quite see 'cos it were that dark . . . and at the end when the lights were coming on again . . . they looked right soft and embarrassed-like . . . and I could've sworn I heard that Barry Wakefield say to Ann . . . just at the end of *Flash Gordon* . . . in the dark . . . 'e said . . . 'Give us a kiss'.

Barry: . . . I never! It's not true! You don't arf tell lies, Susan Arkwright! I never said it! Never!

Susan: It were something like that! . . . what a hero!

Barry: It wasn't.

Susan: You don't kid me, Barry Wakefield — I heard!

(*She goes*)

Barry: How d'you like that? Mouth like a West Country oven — ears like a fish — and brain the size of a pea. I never said that! She wants lookin' at! She wants her brains washing. Still we heroes have to put up with fools. I may have to save Susan Arkwright from a blazing towering inferno.

Charlie: What did you say to her, then?

Barry: To who?

Charlie: Ann.

Barry: Oh that . . . well . . . I just said . . . well . . . er . . . kiss me Hardy! (*To audience*) Just practising, that's all!

(*Scene: in the Washeteria: the cast make a 'humming' in the background.*)

Neighbour 1: I was in the Park you see — gone to feed the ducks.

Neighbour 2: The ducks?

Neighbour 1: When I saw this lad.

Neighbour 2: This lad?

Neighbour 1: He was jumping in and out of the duckpond.

Neighbour 2: The duckpond?

Neighbour 1: I thought . . . here's a funny thing.

Neighbour 2: Funny thing?

Neighbour 1: And I couldn't get me crusts to the ducks properly . . . and I do look forward to feeding them . . . 'cos he was splashing about and that.

Neighbour 2: Splashing?

Neighbour 1: And then I recognised him . . . it was Gladys Wakefield's lad . . .

Neighbour 2: Barry!

Neighbour 1: That's him . . . so I says . . . and what d'you think you're doing, Bernard?

Neighbour 2: Barry!

Neighbour 1: Yes ... and he said ... to me ... he said ...

Neighbour 2 ⎫
⎬ Practising.
Neighbour 1 ⎭

Neighbour 1: How did you know?

(*The 'humming' stops.*)

Neighbour 2: You should see him rescuing cats from trees.

Barry: I know it's only small beginnings ... but they're in the paper every day. Here, listen to this one ...
'BOATING LAKE HERO. Young Tracey Marshall, 6, of Kidderminster Avenue is recovering from her narrow escape from drowning yesterday in the boating lake at Southfield Park. Tracey slipped while playing at the edge and was rescued by Rex, the 8-year-old Alsatian who is a family pet ...' (*He tails off.*)

(*Scene: the School Corridor.*)

Charlie: Are you on careers interview today, Barry?

Barry: Woof! Woof!

Charlie: Morning or afternoon?

Barry: Woof! Woof! Woof!

Charlie: So am I.
Is your mum coming up?

Barry: Woof!

Charlie: No! They don't have to. (*To audience*) He's almost human you know, I think he understands almost everything we say to him. Barry (*He whistles.*) ... walkies!

(*Scene: the School Assembly.*)

Headmaster: Thank you, Mr Barnes. I just want to have a word with you fifth-years about the importance of the Careers interviews that have been arranged for you all today. I'm sure that all of you realise the importance of making the correct decision as regards your career. All too soon the public examinations will be upon us and it is vital that you adopt now the correct attitude to work. For out of these examinations will come the results upon which the career choice that you have made, in conjunction with the Authority's Careers Officers, and our own Careers Teachers − Miss Abbot and Mr Costello − for whose guidance I know you are all immensely grateful − depend! What more can I say?

Barry: 'I see you stand like greyhounds in the slips,
Straining upon the start. The game's afoot:
Follow your spirit; and, upon this charge
Cry "God for Harry! England and . . ."'

Mr Summers: Next.

(*Scene: The Careers Room. Barry walks into careers interview.*)

Mr Summers: Do take a seat, Mushtaq.

Barry: It's Barry!

Mr Summers: Mr Costello has, I know, spoken to you already, Mushtaq . . . and explained the difficulties in a medical career . . .

Barry: I'm Barry! Barry! Not Mushtaq!

Mr Summers: Barry?

Barry: That's right, Barry Wakefield.

Mr Summers: So you're not Mushtaq Ahmed of 5PR?

Barry: That's right — I'm not!

Mr Summers: Wakefield, you say, Wakefield ... Wakefield ... ah here we are ... Wakefield, Barry A.

Barry: Arthur.

Mr Summers: Really?

Barry: After Arthur Fitzgibbon, but his real name was Andrew.

Mr Summers: Really?

Barry: A mistake when he was gazetted.

Mr Summers: So? ... Now! ... Tell me! ... What direction are you thinking of? What ... area, if I may use a technical term, were you aiming for ...

Barry: Heroics.

Mr Summers: Mm! ... Yes ... but what exactly?

Barry: I don't want to be precise ... any aspect, really.

Mr Summers: I see — and what subjects are you studying at present?

Barry: Well ... English and Maths, of course ... and then me options are Art, CDT, PSE, Typing and the Link Course in Electronic Engineering.

Mr Summers: Yes ... well, are there any questions you want to ask me ? ...er ...

Barry: Barry — well, my Mum and Dad wondered if there was a YTS scheme that would be useful. So that I could broaden my knowledge of heroics and ... you know ...

Mr Summers: Quite! Quite! ... just a moment, excuse me a minute ... Mushtaq.

(*He goes*)

Barry: He's gone out either for a quick fag or to talk to Mr Costello.

(*Scene: the School Corridor.*)

Mr Summers: Ah, there you are, Lou, ... could I just have a word?

Mr Costello: It'll have to be quick, I should be in T7 with 4HN.

Mr Summers: About ... Mushtaq ... Wakefield.

Mr Costello: Barry.

Mr Summers: That's him. I'm just interviewing him now.

Barry: Mr Costello will put him right.

Mr Costello: An easy case ... easy! All Barry wants to ...

Mr Summers: Yes! Yes! I know, aerobics! He said!

Barry: Just someone else who doesn't listen.

Mr Costello: Aerobics! No ... you got it wrong ... Heroics ... he wants to be a hero, does our Barry.

(*He goes*)

Barry: Mr Thing never came back. He confirmed all my dad's worst suspicions about Careers Officers.

(*Scene: Barry's Home.*)

Dad: What kind of a job's that? I mean . . . a job advising people about getting a job. How do you train for that? What do they know about real work? Eh?

Barry: And he dashed off to the pub to settle an old score with Basil Rathbone.

Mother: You can't sit there all day, our Barry! I mean it's six weeks since you left school. Heroes should be up and about, seeking employment — that Mr Tebbit says so.

Barry: I've got a puncture.

Mother: I mean, Charlie's got that job down at the joke shop — I saw him in a mask last Monday and he always says 'Hello', and Graham Armitage is working in a bank, and here you are . . . waiting . . . to be a hero. I thought you would have grown out of it by now . . . I really did ! It was nice when you were little, it was different, . . . but now . . . I mean, Barry . . . there just don't seem to be the job opportunities. What are you going to do?

Barry: She had a point there. I mean, I was prepared . . . I was at the ready . . . but there was no demand . . . not round our way. And anyway I didn't find the jokes funny any more.

(*Scene: the Street.*)

Tom: Why not go on one of them YTS schemes, Barry? They need heroes.

Tim: Hey, Barry, why not become religious — you could open your own church — for hero-worship!

Harry: Have you heard about that Hero course at East Anglia University, Barry — posthumous students only!

Larry: Come on the dole with us, Barry — that's where the real heroes are.

Charlie: Why don't you join the Army, Barry? It's a man's life! And it could be your big chance to make hero.

Barry: Of course! Now why didn't I think of that before? The Falkland conflict. (*The cast whistle 'Colonel Bogey'.*) My word yes. *The Bridge on the River Kwai. A Bridge Too Far. All Quiet on the Western Front. Gallipoli. The Long and the Short* and it was only a bus ride down to the recruiting office.

(*Scene: the Bus.*)

Conductor: Fares, please.

Barry: Terminus, please.

Conductor: That'll be 30 pence.

Barry: Half-fare?

Conductor: Who're you kidding? Half-fare? Do you think I was born yesterday? Come off it — pay up or get off — we expect our heroes to be honest, Barry Wakefield.

Barry: I thought Specky Wilkinson wanted to be an engine-driver. How are the mighty fallen!

Conductor: Terminus! Everybody out! You as well, Thomas More.

Barry: I didn't know you did History at School.

Conductor: Literature — *A Man for all Seasons* — get it right Barry Wakefield! It's my tea break now!

Barry: Heroes don't need tea breaks. We have inner strength! It's a sort of Yoga, I suppose. It's meditation. I think therefore I am. That's it. And relax. Relax.

(*Scene: the Recruiting Office.*)

Sergeant: Can I help you?

Barry: What?

Sergeant: Sergeant Grace, . . . can I be of assistance in any way?

Barry: I'd like to join the Army.

Sergeant: I see . . . one moment, I'll call the Captain.

(*He exits.*)

Barry: This is it! Barry! This is it!

Captain: Ah, there you are . . . Mister . . . ?

Barry: Wakefield. Barry Wakefield.

Captain: Splendid! Now my Sergeant here tells me you're interested in joining us. Is that it, Sergeant?

Sergeant: Yes sir!

Captain: What had you in mind?

Barry: Well . . . I thought as how the army has a long and heroic tradition . . .

Captain: 'Heroic' did you say?

Barry: Yes – heroic . . . Charge of the Light Brigade and all that.

Captain: Oh, good heavens, we don't mention that.

Sergeant: No sir!

Captain: Fiendish mistake, you know.

Barry: Well ... Waterloo then ...

Captain: Ah yes ... well ...

Sergeant: Blücher sir!

Captain: Quite ... it was Blücher ... really we just happened to be around.

Barry: What about the Somme?

Captain: Ooh! (*Intake of breath.*) ... No!

Sergeant: Definitely not.

Barry: El 'Alamein.

(*Captain and Sergeant shake heads.*)

Captain: You must realise that the Army of today is a different ...

Sergeant: ... kettle of fish, sir!

Captain: Quite! Attitudes are different, and above all our role is different. However, we can offer you trade-training and the opportunity to travel. Meet new people. Travel to places with exotic names. Just step into my office and I'll outline our procedures to you.

(*The three exit.*)

(*Scene: the Street.*)

Charlie: Charles Taylor: Joke Salesman.

Specky: Robert Wilkinson: Bus Conductor.

(*Charlie echoes 'Engine Driver'.*)

Robbo: Simon Robinson: Games Teacher.

(*Charlie echoes 'Professional Footballer'.*)

Samantha: Samantha Morton: Barmaid.

(*Charlie echoes 'Fashion Model'.*)

Fatty: Edward Wotherspoon: Security Guard.

(*Charlie echoes 'Detective'.*)

Tom: Clown!

Charlie: DHSS Clerk!

Larry: Pop star!

Charlie: Unemployed!

Harry: Vicar!

Charlie: On probation!

Tim: A policeman.

Charlie: A policeman!

Barry: A hero!

Charlie: A soldier.

Barry: 4753261 Wakefield, Barry (*Pause.*) . . . Andrew.

(*He salutes, all freeze.*)

BBC Newscaster (*Recorded voice***):**   . . . but that it was anticipated that the cost of living index would change markedly and for the better before the end of the year.

(*The cast begin singing a reprise of 'Barry, Don't be a Hero' softly and slowly.*)

The Prince and Princess of Wales began a short holiday at
Balmoral today. Crowds of visitors waved them farewell as
the Royal Train pulled out of Paddington Station.

Manchester United continued their successful run of home
wins with a 2-1 defeat of Liverpool earlier tonight. There
seems little possibility that any team in the Canon League
First Division can catch them now.

An off-duty soldier was shot dead in the Lower Falls area
of Belfast tonight. His name is being witheld until next of
kin have been informed.

(*A shot is heard: Barry falls slowly to the ground.*)

And that is the end . . . . . .

(*All cast walk off, leaving Barry lying on the stage.*)

CURTAIN

Activities

Unsung is written to be performed in a drama studio or on a
stage, but it could also be adapted for radio. Before you put on
a performance or make a tape-recording of it, first work
through these exercises.

Thinking about the characters

1 As you read the play, what picture did you build up of
Barry? What is your idea of his physical appearance? For
example, do you see him as tall, short or of average height?
What is his build? What clothes do you picture him wearing?
What would his bedroom be like? What objects would you find

in his room? Jot down your ideas about Barry, then compare them with other people's ideas of him.

2 Work in pairs. Each write a sentence or two summing up what sort of person you think Barry is. Talk about the impression of Barry you would try to create if you were playing the part in a production of the play.

3 What is Barry's idea of a hero? Pick out the references to famous heroes that he makes during the play. Talk about why he wants to be a hero.

4 Talk about how the author, David Foxton, uses Barry as a symbol. He is not just an individual — Barry Wakefield — he also represents thousands of others like him, whose ambition is to make a name for themselves when they grow up.

5 Work with a partner. Make a list of the scenes that occur in the play and write down the names of the characters that appear in each one. Then go through the play scene by scene. Make notes on the behaviour of each of the characters other than Barry and on what their attitude towards Barry is.

6 Write an extra speech to add to the play in which Barry reads out something he wrote during the first year at secondary school, either a composition entitled 'My ambition' or a news report of a heroic deed which he imagines himself having performed.

Thinking about the situations

1 Work in pairs. One of you has just been given the part of Barry in a production of *Unsung*, the other is a reporter for a local radio station. Role-play a scene in which the reporter asks questions about the theme of the play and why it is called

Unsung. Before you begin, make a list of the questions that the interviewer is going to ask.

2 Imagine that a version of *Unsung* has been shown on TV and that later in the evening there is a studio discussion of the play. In threes, role-play a discussion in which a TV presenter talks to two people who saw the play. They discuss what happens in the play and how the play is structured and express their views about it. Before you begin, make a list of the points you are going to include in your discussion.

Further developments

1 Write two monologues to add as a postscript to the play, one in which a former classmate of Barry's reads a report from the local paper which makes out that Barry died a heroic death while serving his country, and another in which an Army colleague, a friend of Barry's who witnessed the shooting, relates what he saw and says that there was nothing heroic or glamorous about Barry's death.

2 Work in a group and devise another scene to add to the play in between two of the existing scenes. Either develop an idea of your own or use one of the following ideas as a starting point:

a) A scene at the hairdresser's when Barry is having his hair cut and the hairdresser asks him about what he wants to do when he is old enough to leave school.

b) A scene at a parents' consultation evening at school when one of the teachers discusses Barry's prospects with his parents.

c) A classroom scene, perhaps during a history lesson about a heroic incident or during a literature lesson in which a story about a hero is being read, in which Barry daydreams of achieving his ambition and becoming a hero. Try out your ideas in improvisations, then write your script and decide where you could fit the scene into the play.

Presenting the play

1 *Unsung* is designed so that it can be presented very easily either in a drama studio or on a stage. No scenery or properties are needed, other than the chairs on which the cast sit in a semi-circle. Similarly, there is no need for the cast to wear costumes. They can wear workshop clothes — a dark top and dark trousers or skirt.

2 The play could be presented as a radio script, but you may feel you need to make some adaptations to it in order to make the scene-changes absolutely clear to the listeners. In pairs, go through the play, listing the scene-changes, then consider each one carefully and decide how you could indicate it. Make any alterations to the script which you think are necessary, then make a tape-recording of it.

Writing your own scripts

1 One of the techniques David Foxton uses in *Unsung* is to make his central character, Barry, address some of his remarks directly to the audience rather than to any of the other characters. Work with a partner and talk about the scenes you might include in a play about a girl or a boy whose ambition is to become a TV star. Then choose one of the scenes and write a script for it. Use the technique of making your main character address some remarks directly to the audience.

2 Develop a script telling the story of a girl or a boy who is determined to succeed at something. Write a scene in which the girl or boy encounters opposition from somebody or an obstacle of some kind, but manages to overcome it.